If These WALLS *Could* TALK:

NEW YORK YANKEES

If These WALLS Could TALK:
NEW YORK YANKEES

Stories from the
New York Yankees Dugout, Locker
Room, and Press Box

Jim Kaat with Greg Jennings

TRIUMPH
BOOKS

Library of Congress Cataloging-in-Publication Data

Kaat, Jim.
    If these walls could talk : New York Yankees : stories from the New York Yankees dugout, locker room, and press box / Jim Kaat, with Greg Jennings.
        pages cm
    ISBN 978-1-62937-024-8
    1. New York Yankees (Baseball team)—History. 2. New York Yankees (Baseball team)—Anecdotes. I. Jennings, Greg. II. Title.
    GV875.N4K32 2015
    796.357'64097471--dc23
                                                                2014036446

This book is available in quantity at special discounts for your group or organization. For further information, contact:

Triumph Books LLC
814 North Franklin Street
Chicago, Illinois 60610
(312) 337–0747
www.triumphbooks.com

Printed in U.S.A.
ISBN: 978-1-62937-024-8
Design by Amy Carter
Photos courtesy of Getty Images

To all the people behind the cameras, in the truck, and behind the scenes that make my job the easiest job in the world.

And to Margie, my Energizer Bunny wife who keeps me young and healthy.

To Chris Pfeiffer, for having the audacity to put us two authors together.

And to Russ and Carole, Kelly, Kortney, Madison, and Gavin. Without you guys there are no words.

CONTENTS

FOREWORD

The New York Yankees are...different. I'm sure I'm not the first person to utter those words, but after playing on five teams in two leagues in three different decades I can say, definitively, that they are *different*. I joined the team in 1995 at the trade deadline. I'd left the Mets in '92 for a short stint in Toronto and followed that with a couple of years in Kansas City before heading back to Toronto. I still had my apartment from my Mets days and at that point in my career I needed to feel what it was like to be a Yankee. Blue Jays president Paul Beeston knew of my desire, he worked out a deal with George Steinbrenner, and I was on my way back to the Big Apple.

I was going to a ballclub that hadn't seen a postseason since the first year of the Reagan Administration. But the honor of putting on that iconic pinstriped uniform with no name on the back of the jersey, the chance to take the field where more baseball history has been written than anywhere else on Earth, the thrill of playing in front of thousands of fans who can trace their devotion back generations—I was ready for it. Or at least I thought I was.

In '95 the Yankees clinched the very first American League wild-card berth (add that to a long list of Yankee "firsts") on the last game of the season. The American League Division Series would start two days later in New York. The only thing crazier than the rush to get tickets for the game was the traffic while trying to get to the ballpark. I was the Game 1 starter and left my apartment in Manhattan with plenty of time. I was, after all, ready for this. But I was stuck in dead-stopped traffic on the Major Deegan Expressway still miles from the stadium and the clock ticking down. I began to wonder if I'd even make it to the game on time. Luckily, I was able to flag down a pair of motorcycle cops, who realized who I was and what I was scheduled to do that night. Before I knew it, I had an unofficial escort clearing my way to Yankee Stadium. People in the traffic weren't pleased at first. They were all trying to either get to the stadium or home or a bar to watch the game. But when they realized what the sirens were for, suddenly I was getting serenaded by car horns and shouts of "Go get 'em, Coney!"

I had been to the playoffs twice before—with the Mets in '88 and the Blue Jays in '92 when we went all the way. But this was my first post-season in the Bronx. You learn quickly that there are no fair-weather Yankees fans. (It's a by-product of that whole "love 'em or hate 'em" thing.) Yankees favorite Don Mattingly had performed tirelessly in pinstripes his whole career without ever playing in the postseason. When Donnie came out to run wind sprints before the game, he got a standing ovation from the always knowledgeable fans. I had never seen or heard anything like it and I still get chills thinking about it. We would lose that series in five games to the Mariners. I'd lost in the playoffs before, but knowing that was Mattingly's last shot at a World Series—that one cut a little bit deeper for me.

I played for the Yankees until 2000. We made the postseason every year and won four titles in five years. Not many franchises can put that on their resumes. I then went to the Red Sox and got to see the Yankees from the rivals' perspective. And I ended my career over in Queens with the Mets and got to re-live those crosstown comparisons one more time. From every vantage point I've been fortunate enough to have, I see that the highs are higher and the lows are lower whenever that Yankees uniform is involved. It's just *different.*

I've known Jim Kaat for most of my adult life. And you know what? He's different, too, in a very Yankees sort of way. Our careers overlapped for the briefest of moments in 1983. I was a 20-year-old prospect invited to spring training with the Royals. Jim was in the final season of a 25-year career. Kansas City was playing St. Louis, and as the Royals were taking batting practice, Jim walked on the field. It's hard to miss him. Jim's a big guy and carries himself with a straight-backed quiet confidence you just don't see that often. Think John Wayne with a curveball. And I could see right away the respect the Royals players showed him. George Brett did his best "Kitty" (as Jim is known) impersonation, drawing smiles and laughs from everyone, especially from Jim himself. And you could see that for Brett—the future Hall of Famer—Jim's approval mattered. At that early stage in my career, I hadn't met too many ballplayers who could command respect like that. Looking back now more than 30 years later, I can say I still haven't.

Jim was a pitching coach for a few seasons with the Cincinnati Reds back in the mid-1980s. While I never saw much of him in that capacity, I was exposed to his pitching philosophy through guys like John Franco, who played for Jim in Cincinnati. For Kitty, pitching was all about rhythm and timing. And while he believed in throwing every day, he saw no use in running his pitchers. He thought that worked muscles you don't use while pitching. He used to say you'd be better off taking the time you spent running and spend it on a dance floor. And he was only half kidding. When I walked out to the mound for one of my starts, some of Jim's teachings went with me.

For my entire Yankees career, Jim was up in the booth. And once again Jim's way of doing things set him apart from other broadcasters. While games were being played, the Yankees broadcasts were always on the TV back in the clubhouse. And players would often sneak back there to watch some of it. It wasn't because they wanted to see how we looked on TV. It was because they wanted to hear what Jim was saying. He might be giving information on a particular player or situation. Or if something unusual happened in the game, you'd always hear somebody say, "What did Kitty have to say about that?" And players would pass that information around. It was almost like getting notes in class. Players were using Jim and his knowledge of the game to improve their own. It was unlike anything I had seen before or since.

I am a broadcaster, myself, these days. And I love my job. But I think I love it more because of Jim. I had the unbelievably good fortune to work my very first telecast with Kitty. It was 2002, and the Mets were playing the Yankees in an interleague game. I was joining Jim and Michael Kay on the YES Network. After seeing the high regard players had for him as a broadcaster and player, I have to admit it was a little intimidating going into that booth. I was a little nervous, but I had no reason to be. Jim was incredibly generous and so easy to work with. He taught me the timing of a broadcast, how to let the game come to me and fit any stories or information I had into the flow of the game and not force it. He made it so enjoyable that I'm still doing it to this day.

So if you stopped me on the street and asked me, "David, who do you think would be great at telling a bunch of Yankees stories that would give the best fans in the world a unique look inside the greatest franchise in history of sports?" I would give you a list—with a single name on it, and that name would be Jim Kaat. You might then look at me and say, "A list with one name on it? Well, that's sort of...*different*." To which I'd reply, "Yes, it is absolutely, positively—and somehow perfectly—different."

—David Cone

INTRODUCTION

My playing career stretched across seven presidential administrations—from Eisenhower to Reagan. My announcing career intersected another five—Reagan to Obama. I was fortunate to pitch in 898 major league games for the Washington Senators, Minnesota Twins, Chicago White Sox, Philadelphia Phillies, St. Louis Cardinals, and, of course, the New York Yankees. I started for more than 600 of those contests, and my teams won 345 of those starts. I even had the opportunity to start a game for the Yankees when I was 40 years old, and we won that game.

The paths I've crossed, the people I've played with and against, those I've worked with or watched in action, all of them have given me a broad and unique perspective on the boys in the Bronx. And after all that time, I still consider myself a student of the game. I've never lost my curiosity or love of baseball. My eyes are always open to see something new. A question is always poised on the tip of my tongue. Obviously the walls of Yankee Stadium have seen more than any living soul, and if they *could* talk, I'd be sitting there right in the front row ready to listen and learn.

As a former Yankees opponent, player, and announcer, let me take you into the Yankees' inner sanctum. From the Babe to the magical 1961 season to the Bronx Zoo, which I experienced firsthand, to the Core Four dynasty, which I broadcast, many of the best stories in the game involve the boys in pinstripes. And that's no surprise, considering they won 27 World Series. Sure, there are some anecdotes that have been repeated so many times that they border on myth. But there are others that have hardly made the rounds. And still more that have never seen the light of day. You will find all three kinds within these pages. With any luck you will read something here on Yogi, the Mick, Catfish, Sweet Lou, Donnie Baseball, Tino, the Boss, etc. and want to pass it on to the next generation of Yankees fans. Sprinkled in are tales from the broadcast booth and how I go about my job, which is often less glamorous than it looks—but also more complicated.

I make my Yankees debut during the seventh inning at Yankee Stadium against the California Angels on May 12, 1979.

I have spent more than three quarters of my life around professional baseball. And in all that time I have met very few people who like the Yankees. I've met thousands who absolutely love them. People whose family histories are punctuated with where they were when Mickey retired or Reggie hit three out or Jeter did something Jeter-esque. And I've met plenty of folks who hate the Yankees with a passion. Ones who have two favorite teams, the second being whomever is playing the Yankees. And yet even the haters respect the team. The late George Steinbrenner was born and raised a Cleveland Indians fan. But when he was a kid, whenever the Yankees came to town, he never missed a chance to watch them walk through their hotel lobby. Even then he knew there was something different about these guys. But in all my travels I've found nary a soul who simply likes the Yankees. They are one of the few teams in all of sports that have no middle ground. No half measures. When it comes to the Yankees and Yankees fans, it's all or nothing. Love or hate. And that makes them a very interesting subject to write about.

—*Jim Kaat*

CHAPTER 1
THE BATTERY

I've always considered myself fortunate to have had a major league career that spanned four different decades. I got to play for six different teams across both leagues and won 283 games during my 25 seasons. But even with all that mileage, I'll never forget my first victory. It came at Yankee Stadium. And I watched it happen…from the stands.

It was April 27, 1960. I had been called up by the Washington Senators at the end of the previous season and made the team out of spring training. It was my second start of the year. (I had left my first start with a one-run lead over Boston in the eighth inning, but the Red Sox came back to win.) So here I was, all of 21 years old, still wet behind the ears, taking the mound at perhaps the most famous sporting venue in the world. And I was going up against legendary Yankees lefty Whitey Ford.

By this point in his career, Whitey had made five of his eventual 10 All-Star Game appearances and collected four of his six World Series rings. His Cy Young Award and World Series MVP performance were still a year away. And though he stood only 5'10", to my 6'4" frame, I couldn't help but feel I was taking on a giant.

Back then, pitchers warmed up at Yankee Stadium in the area adjacent to home plate. As a lefty, when I went into my "stretch" position, I would be looking straight into the Yankees dugout, where I could see Mantle, Berra, Howard, Skowron, all these famous players, and I couldn't help thinking, *It's like looking at the greats from my bubble gum trading card collection—only this time they are staring back at me!* It was rather intimidating, to say the least.

In seven innings I gave up four runs—three of them unearned. Moose Skowron got me for a solo homer in the bottom of the seventh. But in the top of the eighth, the Senators' Jim Lemon hit one out to give us a 5–4 lead. By then I was out of the game but still the pitcher of record. Back in those days, they didn't have us sit in the dugout and ice our arms after pitching. We were just sent off to the showers so we wouldn't stiffen up. I showered and got dressed, but I couldn't sit back there in the clubhouse not knowing what was going on out on the field. So I snuck out into the stands and watched the rest of the game with the fans (all 3,745 of them). Pedro Ramos pitched two innings of relief to get the save. But it was the skinny kid from Zeeland, Michigan, who got the W, his first in the big leagues. And my victory came in the House That Ruth Built.

While that spring day was more than 50 years ago now, I can still remember it like it was yesterday. Of course, baseball history goes back another 100 years past my entry into the box scores. One of the old, nostalgic terms you hear around the game is that of "the Battery." This refers to the pitcher and catcher, but no one knows for sure how it came into use. Some say it was a military reference adopted in the early days of the game. Others have suggested it had something to do with the telegraph and its sender and receiver. But no matter where it came from, one thing is for sure: the pitcher and catcher make a distinct team within a team on the diamond.

Pitchers are a different lot. That's not a bad thing, but if there is a different drummer out there, you can bet the guy marching behind him probably throws a mean curve. Pitchers have to be clever and fearless. Being a little bit crazy doesn't hurt either. The only reason I got to spend parts of two seasons in pinstripes was because of the actions of a pair of great Yankees hurlers. One applied his wits; the other used his fists.

Rich "Goose" Gossage was one of the best relievers in Yankees history. A Hall of Famer, he trails only current Giants pitching coach Dave Righetti and the great Mariano Rivera in saves. Goose even has a better ERA than both of them. At 6'3", 220 and with that biker's moustache, he was an intimidating sight on the mound. And he was as tough as they come. Almost two-thirds of his 310 career saves required Goose to pitch two or more innings. That's unheard of in today's game.

Of course, that tough, ornery edge could also get him in trouble when he wasn't on the mound. Before a game in April of 1979, Goose and backup catcher/designated hitter Cliff Johnson were joking around in the clubhouse. At some point the teasing got to be too much, and the two friends stopped throwing barbs and started throwing punches. Gossage got the worst of it, damaging the thumb on his pitching hand and landing him on the disabled list for months. (A case, though, could be made for Johnson getting the worst part. He would be traded to the Cleveland Indians around the time Goose was coming off the DL.) So now the two-time defending champion Yankees had a problem. They had traded Sparky Lyle away in the offseason, and now Gossage was down for a few months. They needed a closer, and good ones are rarely available early in the season. That's when Ron Guidry stepped up.

"Gator," as Guidry was called, was a phenomenal athlete. Just like Rivera, he probably could've played center field if you needed him to. Guidry was an example of a little guy who could throw hard, and everybody used to wonder how he could do it. It all came down to his upbringing. He did a lot of manual labor as a kid growing up in Louisiana, and that gave him big, strong upper back muscles. It allowed him to throw probably the best slider from a left-handed pitcher that I had seen since Steve Carlton. Guidry said he'd go to the bullpen while Goose healed. He was a much better starter, but this was what his team needed, so he did it. George Steinbrenner lauded Guidry's team-first attitude, saying he wished every Yankees player had the same approach, "First he's for the Yankees, second he's for Guidry." Now the Yankees were scouring around trying to find a lefty to eat up some innings while Gator was the closer. And while I was no Guidry or Gossage, I was a solid stopgap solution—a veteran left-handed pitcher in the bullpen. So if not for a bad punch and a good teammate, I might never have seen how I looked in pinstripes.

I played alongside some great Yankees pitchers during my short stint in the Bronx. But I saw some great ones from the booth as well—guys like Roger Clemens, Randy Johnson, David Cone, Doc Gooden, Andy Pettitte, David Wells, Kenny Rogers, Kevin Brown, Mike Mussina, and

Rivera. I got to witness no-hitters, perfect games, record-breaking performances and I know that a few of these guys are well on their way to being Hall of Famers. But pitchers are a funny lot. Anyone who's been hit by a baseball knows: to stand a mere 60 feet, six inches from someone trying to smash that leather sphere in your direction at a high rate of speed, you have to be cut from different cloth. Fans got to see and become familiar with the various pitching styles of the Yankees hurlers. But seeing them day in and day out over the course of a season or a career as I did, you get a good look at their personalities. And the Yankees definitely had some personalities.

I remember Randy Johnson's first game with the Yankees. The Big Unit was a huge offseason acquisition for the Yankees in 2005, coming over from the Arizona Diamondbacks for Javier Vazquez, Brad Halsey, Dioner Navarro, and some cash. Johnson was the Opening Day starter for the Yankees on April 3. He squared off against the former Yankees pitcher, Wells. The game didn't turn out to be the pitchers' duel most expected. Johnson went six innings, giving up one run on five hits with a half dozen strikeouts and a pair of walks. Wells only lasted four and third, surrendering four runs on 10 hits, and the Yankees cruised to a 9–2 victory.

After the game I was complimentary of Johnson's performance, saying he did well, even though he didn't throw as hard as we kind of expected he would. It was an observation that didn't raise a single eyebrow when I made it. Well, word of this compliment got back to Johnson, but he didn't take it the way it was intended. The next day Johnson cornered my announcing partner, Michael Kay, and said, "Who's your partner, and what is he talking about—'I didn't throw hard enough.' I don't get my good fastball until June!"

When I heard this, my first thought was, *For $16 million a year, you better have your good fastball in April.* But then I realized; Randy had no idea who I was. He didn't realize I had pitched for 25 years. So he thought this was someone talking about a subject they knew nothing about. I guess I would be upset by that, too. But that wasn't the case here.

It is something I have experienced several times as a former player turned broadcaster. You are a member of the media, but your expertise comes from experience, not from books or watching video. A lot of young players quite frankly don't even know you played or what kind of player you were. It's just the way it is today. I can't fathom that happening back in the day. When I saw pitchers like Ford or Warren Spahn or Robin Roberts—and not just the Hall of Famers but all the players—I knew immediately who they were and what they did. I followed the history of the game. Some players still do, but they are in the minority.

Johnson was in New York for two seasons, but I found him hard to connect with. He could often be aloof and rude. At times you didn't even want to approach and talk to him. Then there would be these other moments where he'd speak to you in a genial way and you'd find yourself thinking, *Is this the same guy? Does he know he's talking to me or does he think I'm someone else?* But those moments were few and far between. At the end of the 2006 season, he asked to be traded back to Arizona. His brother had recently passed away, and he wished to be closer to his family. Yankees general manager Brian Cashman complied, and thus ended my experience with the Big Unit.

Mussina was another interesting one. He played for the Yankees from 2001 through 2008. He was a five-time All-Star and won seven Gold Gloves on his way to 270 wins. He had all the tools of a great player and is probably as aloof and distant a pitcher on any team that I ever covered. "Moose"—as he was known—went to Stanford and was a very bright guy. But he kind of gave the impression that since he had gone to a prestigious school—that the rest of us were total dummies. Our careers overlapped six seasons in the Bronx, but Mussina never gave me the time of day. A polite "hello" once in a while, maybe. One time, I made him an offer. I recognized from my experience some of the issues he was going through as a pitcher. He had a stretch where he wasn't doing well, and I could relate to that. So I told him I'd be happy to sit down and talk with him about it, pitcher to pitcher. He looked at me like I had three heads. He could also be quite sarcastic. One day I was walking through the clubhouse when I heard Mike say, "Oh, the door must be open to the media." I turned and saw him staring right at me, inferring I was not a former player—just a member of the media.

But Johnson and Mussina were the exception with the Yankees, not the rule. Jack McDowell, I think, has changed a great deal now but was cantankerous and distant. But guys like Pettitte and Cone were just the opposite. They always showed me and other former players the respect you show someone who has been through the same trials. I used to take Pettitte, Rogers, and Jimmy Key—an all-lefty foursome—out golfing when we were out on the road. Mike Stanton was great, very professional. So was John Wetteland. So many pitchers during my time with the Yankees were very approachable and easy to talk to, even on the day they were pitching.

That wasn't the case with Clemens.

After 13 years with the hated Red Sox and a pair of buffer years in Toronto, the Rocket came to New York in 1999. He was a major talent in a major market, and when he was pitching, it was a story. But if you tried to talk to him on those days, well, he'd want to bite your head off. In case you slept through the mid-to-late-2000s, Roger was one of several players accused of using anabolic steroids in the 400-plus pages of the Mitchell Report back in December of '07. Clemens denied those allegations under oath before Congress. That denial led to felony perjury charges. And, after almost two years and an intervening mistrial, Roger was cleared of the perjury charges. That's what the lawyers will tell you about the Rocket. Those of us who followed the Yankees and Roger say something else. It was pretty obvious that there was some sort of "rage" going on with Roger that fueled his combative personality. Once Major League Baseball began testing for steroids in 2003, Roger became a leaner, more fit individual. And he became more pleasant to be around and talk to. Coincidence?

Perhaps. All I know is that at the time of this writing, Roger and his 354 wins are on the outside of Cooperstown looking in.

Someone who won't have to wait long to get into the Hall of Fame is Rivera. Mariano arrived in the Bronx in 1995, the same year I started calling games for MSG Network. He came up as a starting pitcher, but he would go on to become the most dominating closer of all time, a 13-time All-Star, and a five-time World Series champion. His 652 career saves are the best in baseball. His remarkable postseason ERA of 0.70 is also the lowest ever. No wonder they called him "Sandman." When he came in, it was like saying good night to the other team.

With such an accomplished resume you might think Rivera would be hard to approach. Nothing could be further from the truth. He was always easy to talk to and a pleasure to be around. I never asked players for autographs for personal gain, but there were a lot of charities that had asked me if I could help them out with some signed items to raise money. I knew I could approach Mariano and say, "Could you sign a baseball to put up for auction for this charity?" And he'd never have a problem with it. Neither would Derek Jeter, Cone, Pettitte, Paul O'Neill, or Bernie Williams. But I never thought of going to Johnson or Mussina.

Cone was another great one. Coney is still one of the only pitchers in that era I can think of who wasn't a robot. He didn't have a cookie cutter delivery, wasn't just a mechanical thinker or pitcher. He was creative and unconventional, a great example of pitching as art instead of a science.

I will never forget Cone's valiant effort in Game 5 of the American League Division Series in Seattle back in 1995. The Yankees led 4–2 in the bottom of the eighth inning when Ken Griffey Jr. homered off of Coney to make it 4–3. You could see right then Cone was really out of gas, but he pitched on. Two walks and a single would load the bases with two out. If they knew how good Mariano would become, then he would have been brought in to start the inning. But this was Mariano's rookie year when he was used mostly as a starter. They wouldn't start converting him to a closer until two seasons later. Buck Showalter and the Yankees brass had lost confidence in Wetteland, so the bullpen was in a state of confusion at this point. Cone fell victim to that. He had done his job, had thrown well over 100 pitches by this point. He didn't deserve to be left out there in that situation. But as a young manager, Showalter's hands were tied because of George's influence on how he was supposed to manage the bullpen. If the same situation happened today, Coney would probably have won that game.

Instead, after a long season and seven and two-thirds stressful innings, Coney is out there trying to get Doug Strange out, pitch after pitch. Finally, on pitch No. 147, a split-fingered fastball misses, and Strange gets the bases-loaded walk to tie the game. That's when Buck brings Rivera in, and he gets a strikeout to end the inning. The game would go to extra innings and was eventually won by Edgar Martinez with his double down the left-field line in the bottom of the 11th. The real hero of the game was the winning pitcher for Seattle—Randy Johnson. As Cone says in his 2001 book, *A Pitcher's Story*, Johnson came in on one day's rest, risking damage to his career in a contract year, and pitched his heart out for his team. Cone writes, "I can't say enough good things about the man who can perform like that when the price is so high."

This game would have a lasting impact on both franchises. For the Mariners—who had been talking about relocating that year—the win kept the franchise in Seattle. For the Yankees this was Don Mattingly's last chance to play in a World Series. Against Seattle, his only appearance in the postseason in his 14-year career, he batted .417 and drove in two runs in the sixth to give the Yankees that 4–2 lead. Donnie Baseball would end his spectacular career in pinstripes without ever playing in the Fall Classic.

Another pitcher who was a treat to be around was Wells. Boomer had two stints with the Yankees: 1997 and '98 and then again from 2002 to '03. He won 239 games over a career spanning 21 seasons. He could get angry with coaches and some teammates and even Joe Torre.

David Wells' teammates lift up the pitcher after he throws the 15th perfect game in Major League Baseball history. Wells later claimed he performed the feat while hung over. *(AP Images)*

Sometimes he annoyed them because he'd react when a play wasn't made behind him. He'd kind of show up the player who made the error. But he was probably my favorite player while doing a game because you knew when Boomer took the mound he was going to be in a good rhythm. He worked fast, threw strikes, and wasn't going to take a lot of time between pitches. His games always had a nice flow to them.

One of the coolest things I saw Wells do happened during his second season in the Bronx. It was May 17, 1998. Boomer took the mound and proceeded to pitch the 15th perfect game in major league history, beating one of my old teams, the Minnesota Twins, 4–0. Although that was a remarkable feat, it wasn't the best part. That came after the game.

Wells was, of course, the big story that day and hung out for hours talking to reporters about his remarkable achievement. When the media finally had their fill, David headed out to the players' parking lot where he ran into some of his friends from the NYPD who guard the players' cars during games.

You would think that all he'd want is to get out of there and celebrate his perfect game. Not Boomer. He chatted with the officers a bit and then asked, "You guys want to take some batting practice?" After the officers responded with stunned nods, Wells led them down under the stadium into the cages and threw batting practice to these guys *after throwing a perfect game.* That's the kind of guy Boomer was.

Wells also claimed in his 2003 fittingly titled autobiography, *Perfect I'm Not! Boomer on Beer, Brawls, Backaches and Baseball*, that he was pretty darn hung over when he pitched his perfect game. He said he stayed out until 5:00 AM at a *Saturday Night Live* cast party. Some have called that claim into question (citing Wells' ability to embellish stories); others have called it downright irresponsible. Knowing Boomer the way I do, I wouldn't be surprised one bit if he pitched that game hung over.

Perfect in Pinstripes Until David Wells, the only Yankee to pitch a perfect game was Don Larsen, who threw his in Game 5 of the 1956 World Series against the Brooklyn Dodgers. But Boomer and Don had something else in common. They both graduated from the same high school: Point Loma High in San Diego, California. Fourteen months after Wells' bit of perfection, David Cone would add a third perfect game to the Yankee record books. It came on July 18th, 1999, which also happened to be Yogi Berra Day at Yankee Stadium. Yogi caught the ceremonial first pitch to start the game—a pitch thrown by his old battery mate, Don Larsen.

By the time of Boomer's bit of perfection, I had already had some experience with hitless games. In 1996 Gooden signed as a free agent with the Yankees. He broke in with the other New York team in 1984 and in his first three years with the Mets he won Rookie of the Year, a Cy Young, and a World Series ring. But his last few years were not so good, and he was struggling so much in the Bronx in April that he was nearly released. But on May 14th, the "Doc" was definitely *in*. Gooden somehow found that old magic and no-hit the Mariners.

I was part of the broadcast team that called that game for MSG Network, and as the game was going on, we never said a word about the no-hitter. There's the old baseball superstition that if you say, "Hey, this guy's throwing a no-hitter," then the next guy gets a hit, and you jinxed him. So we kind of hushed it up. I'd say things like, "If you have friends at home, tell them to turn on the TV. Something special is going on here at Yankee Stadium." But that was about it.

Bob Raissman, the great sportswriter for the *New York Daily News*, watched our coverage of Doc's no-hitter. And while Bob became very supportive of me and I consider him a friend in the media, in this instance he was downright critical of how we had called the game. He took issue with the fact that we didn't notify the viewers what was going on. It's one thing to be superstitious in the dugout, but in the broadcast booth, it has no place. He said that we work for the viewer, so we have to keep them informed. And as I look back, I can honestly say I didn't really do that. So the criticism was correct. I should not have followed the superstition. Oddly enough, a few months later we won a New York Emmy for our coverage of the Gooden no-hitter. So we were rewarded and chastised for our coverage of the same game. You gotta love New York.

Fast-forward to Boomer's perfect game in '98. After he got the first six Twins hitters out, I could still hear Raissman's criticism in my ear. So we began to talk about seven in row, then eight in a row. The heck with the taboo, we were going to tell the fans what was going on. And it was great. You can kind of feel that tension and anxiety building among the fans in the stands. That made that game much more enjoyable, covering it that way because you were building the story pitch-by-pitch, out-by-out instead of hiding and keeping it quiet as players do in the dugout. There was no Emmy for that one but a much more enjoyable experience.

I also watched a perfect game from the dugout, though that one wasn't as enjoyable because it was from the losing side. The year was 1968. I was still playing for the Twins at the time. It was the ninth perfect game in baseball history, and it was thrown by Oakland A's ace, Jim "Catfish" Hunter. Eleven years later, I played alongside Cat. What I remember most about him is how he helped make the bus rides—one of the most mundane things in baseball—one of the highlights of my Yankees career.

With Catfish on board, bus rides in 1979 were priceless. The stories and jokes came out of him faster than his pitches in his prime. I couldn't keep up. When the candy bar of boastful star Reggie Jackson famously debuted, Jim said: "Open it up, and it tells you how good it is." Asked why he never pitched another perfect game, he replied, "The sun don't shine on the same dog's ass all the time." I never pitched a perfect game, but I wish I had—just so I could use that line.

The only player who could keep up with Catfish was Lou Piniella. Back in those days, the Yankees had crowds wherever they went. When they came to town, there would be fans following our bus back to the hotel from the stadium. One time in Kansas City, we saw this pickup truck pulling up alongside. And as we looked out the window, there were two rather large ladies in the back of the pickup, and they were mooning the bus.

Well, Catfish had brought his nine-year-old son, Todd, on this trip with him. And Sweet Lou was sitting right behind them. As we were taking in the "unique" sights Kansas City had to offer, Lou tapped Catfish on the shoulder. "Hey, Jim, at least now when Todd goes back to school, he'll have a nice story for show and tell."

Everyone wants to know how he got the nickname. The story goes that when the scout from the Kansas City A's went to the Hunter family farmhouse to sign him, Jim was out fishing. The scout waited and waited until finally he came home with a string of catfish. It's a great story… but completely fabricated. In truth, Charlie Finley, the owner of the A's, wanted his crop of young ballplayers all to have catchy nicknames to make them more marketable. But it didn't bother Jim at all. In fact he used it to his advantage. Early on in his career, since the name didn't come from his childhood, his old friends only called him Jim. So if someone was trying to get his attention, and they were yeling, "Hey, Catfish," he didn't turn around. He knew they didn't really know him.

Jim, of course, was the first big money free agent in baseball history when he won an arbitration case against Finley in 1974. He was courted by just about every team in baseball but signed with the Yankees for five years and $3.75 million, an astronomical sum in those days. By the time I got to the Bronx, Cat was in the last year of his contact and he wasn't pitching too well. He had been recently diagnosed with diabetes and he was going out there on fumes really. He was getting lit up pretty good. And Piniella would ride him. "Come on, Cat," he'd say. "They put guys in jail for stealing $35 from a 7–Eleven. You're stealing all George's money and walking around like a free man. Why don't you give it up?"

But Cat could give as good as he got. I remember him sitting in the corner of the dugout one time when we were playing the Twins. It was a hot summer's day, but Cat had a towel around his neck like it was cold. That day Piniella was hitting against soft-tossing lefty, Geoff Zahn, and as Lou came back into the dugout after striking out, Cat said, "Man, Lou, the drafts from your swings…I'm freezing all the way over here in the corner of the dugout." It was never a dull moment with those two. Cat retired after the '79 season, an eight-time All-Star with five World Series rings (three with Oakland, two with New York) and a Cy Young. He was inducted into the Hall of Fame in 1987. Sadly, he was diagnosed with ALS, Lou Gehrig's disease, in 1998 and died a year later. Steinbrenner credited Catfish with teaching the Yankees "how to win" in the '70s. But it was his old verbal sparring partner, Piniella, who said it best. "When you play with a guy like that...you feel blessed."

As long as we are going down memory lane, there was another Yankees pitcher I knew very well who made perhaps the biggest impact on pitching since the invention of the curveball. But it wasn't for anything he did on the mound. It was what he did at the doctor's office.

Tommy John and I go back to the mid-1960s, when he was playing for the White Sox and I was still pitching for the Twins. We'd be in Chicago, and I would pitch a night game and the next day I would go down to the bullpen to do some throwing. And T.J. would be doing his laps around the field and he'd stop and say, "What are you doing throwing today, Jim? You pitched nine innings yesterday." That was the conventional wisdom in those days—pitch a day then rest for a couple days. But I was trained differently by Eddie Lopat and Johnny Sain, so I was kind of a throwing freak back then. I probably threw more than any pitcher in baseball because over my quarter century in the big leagues. I did some throwing almost every day.

Jump ahead to the '70s, and T.J. underwent the now-famous Tommy John surgery to repair a torn ulnar collateral ligament in his elbow. When Dr. Frank Jobe did that first procedure back in '74, he wasn't sure if it would work. He just knew that Tommy would never pitch again if he didn't have it. So Tommy rolled the dice and had the surgery and in doing so he changed the game. Now more than 500 major league pitchers have had it. Some big names like John Smoltz, Orel Hershiser, Eric Gagne, and Stephen Strasburg all had their careers extended because T.J. was willing to be a guinea pig.

The first time I bumped into Tommy after his surgery, he said, "Wouldn't you know it, the first thing Dr. Jobe told me to do...He said 'Once that elbow heals up, you start playing catch *every* day.'" His wife,

Sally, was even his catcher in the backyard for soft-toss sessions. Tommy and I got to be teammates briefly in '79 with the Yankees, and we did our throwing together all the time. We were the only two who would do that.

These days I still kid Tommy that a lot of people hear "Tommy John surgery" and think he's a doctor. Dr. Jobe passed away in March of 2014. Now it seems like Dr. James Andrews and Dr. David Altchek, the Mets orthopedic surgeon, are the go-to doctors for this proceedure. The success rate is still around 75 percent that the pitchers will come back as good or better after the procedure. And most of the UCL surgeries performed these days are on high school or college pitchers. It all starts with tiny microtears when kids are little league age and pitching too often and trying to throw too hard before the bones and muscles and ligaments have fully formed. Times sure have changed, haven't they, "Dr. John?"

Ulnar Collateral Damage I might be the only pitcher whose career was "hurt" by the benefits of Tommy John surgery. When I retired in 1983 after 25 seasons, I had the longest career of any pitcher in major league history. Thanks to his famous surgery, Tommy would go on to break my record six years later when he played his 26th season in 1989. But in the end, his stint with the record was even shorter than mine. It ended in 1993, when a fella named Nolan Ryan played his 27th year in the majors.

Pettitte was another great Yankee lefty. I've always had a special spot for Andy. I met him when he came up in 1995. Billy Connors, the pitching coach at the time, had me talk to Andy a little bit about pitching. I always looked at Andy as a clone of myself. He could do a lot more things with a baseball at a young age than I. But we had similar builds. We were both 6'4" to 6'5" and 220 to 230 pounds. I had the fastball and curveball, but I never developed the cutter or change-up he did. And I never had the exposure of pitching for the Yankees in the postseason like he did. But our motions and approaches to pitching were quite similar. It was fun to watch his career from the booth and to see what a great pitcher he developed into. But there was one game he pitched that I'll never forget.

It was August 24, 1998. The Yankees were playing the Angels at Yankee Stadium. Andy was pitching and was rolling along with a comfortable lead, when all of a sudden, the Angels started putting a couple hits together. Our first-base cameraman for MSG Network, Dave Chesney, was really sharp and was always great at finding things that would have an impact on game. From his viewpoint he could look into the visiting team's dugout and he saw Angels batting coach Rod Carew talking to Wally Joyner and the other hitters with a baseball in his hand. And he was spinning and holding it in such a way that it made me think that Rod had picked up something from Andy's pitches by the way he gripped the ball. There are several ways to do this. Maybe the pitcher shows a lot of white on the curveball or the fastball, or maybe his arm angle changes. Whatever it was, Carew—one of the great hitters from my era—was picking it up and was relaying it to Angels hitters. So I said on the air, "It looks like the Angels have found something, and they are able to pick up the pitches that Andy Pettitte is throwing." It was simply an observation of what I was seeing on the monitors and what was unfolding in the game in front of me. (This issue of tipping his pitches would come back to haunt Pettitte and the Yankees in a big way in Game 6 of the 2001 World Series. Arizona's Jay Bell told *The New York Times* the Diamondbacks figured out what Andy was throwing by the way he held his glove. They went on to win that game 15–2 and the series in seven games.)

Well, as I was saying this, my good friend Chili Davis, who was with the Yankees at that time, was back in the clubhouse and hears me on the TV talk about how to tell what a pitcher is throwing. He then returns to the dugout and says, "Kitty is on TV telling the audience that he's got

Pettitte's pitches, that he can tell when he's throwing a curve or a fastball. And the Angels must be listening and they are acting on it!"

In reality the Angels were on to it before I was. They would use this tactic to help them score five runs in the sixth inning and go on to win the game. The Yankees, needless to say, weren't happy. And while nothing was said to the press, I did get wind of some heated words (off the record) that were directed toward me.

The next day I get a call from our producer Leon Schweir. He said, "Joe Torre wants to see you." So I went down to Joe's office, and he couldn't have been nicer. He immediately said, "I watched the tape. You didn't say anything wrong. I don't know why those guys got so heated about that." I was glad to hear that Joe knew what I had done and that I had not given the Angels an advantage. But there was definitely a cool atmosphere when I went around the clubhouse that day. Even pitching coach Mel Stottlemyre—a guy I've known and have been friends with for years—wouldn't say a word in my direction. Don Zimmer, however, didn't hesitate to come to my defense. "I've known Jim for 30 or 40 years," he said, "and I guarantee he wouldn't do anything like that." But that wasn't enough for Joe Girardi, who had caught the game. He had some colorful comments—often with my name attached to them.

Later that day, I am back up in the booth, getting ready for the next game. No one had said anything critical to my face, but no one had apologized either. So I went on about my day—business as usual. About 15 minutes before the game, I get a call, which asked me: "Do I have time to go downstairs? Joe Girardi wants to talk." Well, with the slow elevators at the old Yankee Stadium, I wasn't sure I did have time, but I went. I found Joe and was ready to get an earful when he took me aside and said, "I could not start tonight's game without apologizing to you." That surprised me a bit, but he went on. "I finally heard what you said on the air. You didn't do anything wrong. We just got all hot and bothered because of losing that game and reacted in a way that we shouldn't have."

That was very thoughtful of Joe. Though we both had a job to do in mere moments, he didn't want that misunderstanding to fester. And he was the only one to say anything to me. I've known Girardi for 20 years or so now. And I know you won't find a more upstanding, first-class guy than him. Maybe that's why we pitchers like our catchers so much.

Catch as Catch Can

The first time I met a Yankees catcher was way back in 1959. I was playing with the Chattanooga Lookouts, a Double A team in the Southern Association. I had just been knocked around by the Atlanta Crackers during a real rough night on the mound. So here I was, a 19-year-old kid just sitting in front of his locker and thinking about the game, when all of sudden I hear the sound of a bus starting up and pulling out of the parking lot. I look up and I was the only one there in the clubhouse.

I went out in the parking lot, and the bus was gone. So I set about trying to flag down a cab, when I saw this older gentleman striding out toward his car. He looked in my direction and said, "What are you looking for, young man?" I said, "Well, I need to get a ride down to the Henry Clay hotel. I missed the team bus."

"Why don't you come ride with me, then. I'm heading in to downtown Atlanta."

I thanked him and hopped in, and we were about two minutes down the road when he extended his hand and he said, "Bill Dickey, former Yankees catcher. " My first thought was, *Wow, Bill Dickey! I knew about you when I was eight years old!* I didn't say that, but it was right there on the tip of my tongue. I knew he had won seven World Series behind the plate and another six as a coach and manager. He was the guy who taught Yogi Berra the ins and outs of being a stellar major league backstop. His .362 batting average in 1936 was the best ever by a catcher until Joe Mauer surpassed it by three points in 2009. And he was giving me a ride! I managed to keep my cool, and we had a nice conversation. He was there on a scouting mission and stayed after the game to write his reports. If this happened today, he would've finished up early on a computer, and I'd still be trying to catch a cab. But back then it was all by hand, fortunately for me, and it resulted in the unique experience of a young kid trying to make his way in baseball hitching a ride with a Hall of Fame catcher.

The Yankees have had two Hall of Famers behind the plate. The other, of course, is Berra. As player and coach, the man appeared in 21 World Series. I played on teams where the entire roster didn't have that much championship experience. The thing with Yogi is he's just an everyday man whom everybody loves. During my announcing days, he came in the clubhouse unannounced and didn't draw a lot of attention. He was kind of like everybody's grandfather. You could sit down and talk baseball with him. And even though he would kind of mumble everything he said, you could tell he was really paying close attention to the game. Yogi knew his stuff.

I only got to face Yogi a few times when I played because he was a left-handed hitter. Most of the time, Elston Howard, a right-handed bat, would catch against me, and they would play another right-handed hitter in left field. Yogi was a tough out, especially with runners on base. Ted Williams, who knows a thing or two about hitting, called Yogi the game's best clutch hitter. And the backstop could hit just about anything thrown up there. He was the best bad-ball hitter in the game, hands down. And he would really hit it. For Yogi, strikeouts were to be avoided at all costs. You had to get the ball in play. In 1950 Yogi had only a dozen strikeouts in nearly 600 at-bats! Yogi's bad-ball ability at the plate came up a fair amount with the team. One time he was asking Jeter why he chased a high pitch on a 3–2 count. Jeter said, "You swung at those pitches." To which Yogi countered, "Yeah, but I hit those. You don't." Or when Alfonso Soriano was coming up and he was swinging at anything near the plate. Only unlike Yogi his strikeouts were through the roof. So Joe Torre thought Yogi should talk to the young man from the Dominican Republic. Yogi's advice was vintage Yogi: "Well, if you see it, hit it. Sometimes you don't see it. I'd let it go, and then next time, I'd swing at it. I saw it better the next time." Soriano spoke Spanish and a little bit of English. This was his first exposure to Yogi-ish.

Yogi could even have an impact on the game from the stands. After the 14-year feud with George Steinbrenner ended in July of 1999, the Yankees had a Yogi Berra Day at the stadium. The starting pitcher that day was David Cone, and as he warmed up in the bullpen, he experienced something he'd never seen before. Before the game the stands were continuously erupting in cheers as Yogi rode around the field on a golf cart. Cone stopped concentrating on his pitches and took in the scene, even waving at Yogi as he drove by. "I had a tremendous feeling of being a part of the Yankee family, of the tradition," Cone said. It was unlike any warm-up he ever had, "so happy-go-lucky, carefree." What might have been a major distraction turned into a major positive. Coney went out and pitched a perfect game that day. Maybe Yogi should circle the field before every Yankee game.

Entire books have been dedicated to Berra's famous Yogi-isms, so it's hard to break new ground here. But there was wisdom in much of what he said. Like when he explained how it was hard to see the ball in left field of Yankee Stadium late in the fall due to the shadows creeping in with a very succinct, "It gets late early out here." Or when things got tough, he'd simply observe, "If the world were perfect, it wouldn't be." One that I always liked happened at Old Timers' Day at Yankee Stadium. One of the great traditions on that day follows the introduction of the Old Timers in attendance. There is always a moment of silence afterward as they read the names of those members of the Yankee fraternity who passed away over the last 12 months. One year after the names were read, Yogi leaned over to Whitey Ford and said, "I hope I never hear my name on that list." Yogi Berra is more than a baseball icon...he is an American treasure. And it will be a sad day for all of us when we hear his name on that list.

Another legendary Yankee catcher I did face a lot was Howard. Elston broke a lot of new ground in the Bronx. In '55 he became the first African American to play for the Yankees and in '69 the first to coach for them, too. He was so respected that players would say you could go an entire season without ever seeing a pitcher shake off one of his signs. But to me Elston was always a tough out at the plate—tougher than even Mickey Mantle.

Back in July of '67, I'm pitching for the Twins, and we had a 1–0 lead with two outs in the bottom of the ninth when the Mick steps up to the plate. The count gets to 3–1, and Twins catcher Russ Nixon calls time and comes out to the mound. "What do you think about making Mickey try to chase something?" I look over at the on-deck circle and see Elston swinging a pair of bats and say, "I'll take my chances with Mantle." Now in those days, that right-field wall was about three feet high and 344 feet to right center, so it was a very convenient target. And wouldn't you know it, Mickey hit a home run to tie the game. And Elston did end up getting a single, but the real damage he did was make me want to pitch to Mantle because of how well he hit me through the years.

So instead of a win, the game ended in a 1–1 tie because of rain. We played the Yankees again a month later, and I actually lost the game 1–0. I pitched two complete games, gave up two runs, and got a loss and a tie, and all because of my respect for Howard. Now you might think, *It's only one game. What's the big deal?* Well, the Twins actually lost the pennant by a single game that year, so it was a big deal. That's what I remember most about Elston.

In 1994 the short-lived Baseball Network was launched. In the fall I worked some Arizona fall league games to generate a little offseason revenue. John Filippelli, one of the producers, asked if there was anybody out there I knew who was trying to break into the business that I might want to take along. Well, I remember from my Yankee days, that catcher Rick Cerone was interested in getting into broadcasting. So they signed Rick, and he and I went out to Arizona to call some games. It turned out to be a lot of fun because we taped the games. They would play the games at about 2:00 in the afternoon, and the crew would record it all, but there were no commercial breaks. So Rick and I could come in and do the game in about two hours. That left our mornings open to play golf. Rick loved to play golf, so we would play Desert Mountain Golf Course. We even played through Phil Mickelson and his group one day. (Lefty, meet Lefty.) Then we'd go to the park, do the game, and that night we would catch a red eye back East. So we had a nice day and a half of baseball and golf.

Jorge Posada was another successful Yankees backstop. He spent his entire 17-year career in pinstripes, collecting four World Series titles along the way. A converted second baseman, Jorge was known for his switch-hitting ability, his power, and his arm. Jorge's dad was a scout, so he was raised to respect the game and play it with the right attitude. It's important to have guys like that on your team. Jorge was also Joe Girardi's understudy, and that really helped his development. But from Day One, Jorge was always a first-class gentleman.

Jim Leyritz won a pair of titles during his two stints behind the plate in the Bronx. He's best known for a pair of walk-off home runs he hit in the postseason. The first was a blast in the 15th inning in the 1995 American Division League Series against the Mariners. That gave the Yankees a 2–0 series lead. Seattle would win the next three and end the Yankees' postseason run that year. The next year, New York reached the World Series for the first time since 1981. They were facing the Atlanta Braves, who took a 2–1 lead in the series thanks to their outstanding pitching staff. In Game 4 the Yankees fell behind 6–0 early on. If they lost the game, Atlanta would have a stranglehold on the title with their bullpen. In the top of the eighth and with the Yankees trailing by three, Leyritz stepped to the plate—for the first time that night—with two men on. He ran the count to 2–2 and then took Atlanta closer Mark Wohlers deep to left to tie the game at 6. The Yankees would win the game 8–6 in 10 innings to tie the series. They'd then sweep the next two games to claim their first World Series title in 18 years. And an argument can be made that the momentum swung in the Yankees' favor the moment Leyritz swung at Wohlers' pitch.

After the 1996 season, the Yankees traded Leyritz to the Angels. He moved around to several teams before landing with the San Diego Padres in 1998, where he played in the World Series against the Yankees. That's when his postseason heroics in pinstripes really showed because during player introductions in the first game at Yankee Stadium—when the opposing team is typically booed incesently—Leyritz received a standing ovation. The Yankee faithful never forget a player who's helped them win a championship. And I guess you could say Leyritz helped the Yankees win the '98 title as well. He went 0-for-10 at the plate for the Padres during the Yankees' four-game sweep.

Perhaps the most bittersweet memories of my baseball career involve a Yankees catcher. When I joined the team in 1979, Thurman Munson was the captain—the first Yankee captain since Lou Gehrig. I only got a chance to throw to him a few times, but there was a lot to like about Thurman. His toughness comes to mind. He was so banged up that year in '79, but he never complained. And he was a true competitor, always pushing and pulling the team to do better. No wonder they called him "Tugboat." And if you ever wanted someone to come up to the plate for your team with two outs in the bottom of the ninth inning and the game on the line, it was Thurman.

I was 40 when I joined the Yankees and not a particularly hard thrower at that point in my career. Thurman would come up to me and

Thurman Munson, whom I dined with two nights before he perished in a plane crash, chats with his battery mate, Sparky Lyle.

say, "Kitty, we're going to pitch backward. When we have a fastball count, we're gonna throw off-speed stuff. And when we're ahead in the count and the hitter's looking for a breaking ball, we're throwing heat." I'd say, "Well, Tugboat, that's not really pitching backward; that's pitching the right way." So we both enjoyed trying to outthink hitters, and that made it a lot of fun to pitch to him.

When I was with the Chicago White Sox, Bucky Dent, Goose Gossage, and I would frequent an Italian restaurant on the southside of Chicago called Traverso's. Now Bucky and Goose and I were all with the Yankees, but when we played in Chicago, we'd still go out to Traverso's. Well, it turned out that the Traverso brothers—John, Richie, and George—were big fans of Thurman's, and they asked if there was ever any chance we could get Thurman to come out to the restaurant. As it happened, we had a three-game series with the Sox, and on a Tuesday night after the game, I rented a car, grabbed Thurman, Graig Nettles, Goose, and Bucky, and we all went out to eat at Traverso's.

When we got there, we found that they had closed the restaurant for us. It was kind of a little, private dinner for the five of us. We had a great night, and Thurman was in heaven. Mama Traverso cooked him up whatever he wanted. It was an evening to remember. The next night we played the Sox again, and then the team headed back to New York for a couple of days off. Everyone except for Thurman. He headed home to Canton, Ohio, to spend some time with his family. It was hard for Thurman to be away from his wife, Diana, and their three kids, Tracy, Kelly, and Michael. That's why he took up flying and purchased a private plane, so he could get back to Ohio more often during the season.

The next day, Thursday, August 2, 1979, I will never forget. I was in the apartment I rented on Central Park South near 6th Avenue—right near where Mickey Mantle's restaurant used to be. I turned on the TV that afternoon and almost hit the floor when I heard: "Some tragic news to report today. Yankees catcher Thurman Munson died today when the plane he was flying crashed at Akron-Canton Airport in Ohio." *What? Thurman was dead?* I couldn't believe it. I just saw him hours before in Chicago. We'd had that great dinner at Traverso's. It gutted me, as it did for the whole team. In an instant the heart and soul of our team was gone.

The entire Yankees organization was in shock from the tragedy. But just as hardship never stopped Tugboat, we knew he wouldn't want this to stop us. On August 3 we started a four-game set with the Batimore Orioles at Yankee Stadium. Before the game started, the Yankees ran on to the field and took their positions. But the catcher's position remained empty. As the players stood there solemnly, there was a moment of silence, a prayer, and Robert Merrill sang "America the Beautiful." Then it was the fans' turn. They all got on their feet and gave Thurman a standing ovation that seemed to last forever. It was a very moving and emotional moment. Finally, Jerry Narron, the man who would take over behind the plate for the Yankees, took the field, and the game began.

Of course, with the passing of Thurman, that pretty much ended the rest of the season for the Yankees. It was a very tragic time, and yet those few months that I got to know and play with Thurman are ones I'll never forget.

The organization never forgot Thurman either. Despite a very crowded clubhouse, Munson's final locker was never reassigned. The empty locker with Munson's No. 15 on it could be found next to Derek Jeter for many years up until the original Yankee Stadium closed in 2008. You can now see Munson's locker at the New York Yankees Museum inside the new stadium.

Nothing happens on the baseball field until the two members of the battery do their thing. But once they do, anything can happen. The ball can go absolutely anywhere. The next closest players to the action at home plate are the first and third basemen, and that's where we'll head next on our trip around the diamond.

CHAPTER 2
THE CORNERS

"I want to know what's the fellah's name on first base."
"What's the fellah's name on second base."
"I'm not asking you who's on second."
"Who's on first."
"I don't know."
"He's on third."

— *Abbott and Costello*

With all due respect to the comedic genius of Bud Abbott and Lou Costello, you definitely want to know who you have on first and third. Other than the pitcher, these two players are the closest targets in the line of fire. That means they usually have the least amount of time to react. So they have to be quick. But often, especially in the modern game, they're called upon to produce at the plate in terms of home runs and RBIs. In the real world, the requirements of being lightning quick as well as strong and powerful tend to be mutually exclusive. So when someone can do both, you know you have a special first or third baseman.

The most famous first baseman to ever play the game wore pinstripes. Lou Gehrig was a blend of immense talent with tremendous humility. He played the first part of his career batting behind the Babe and the latter behind Joe DiMaggio and yet he still averaged 147 RBIs a year for his career. When asked if he minded playing in the Babe's shadow, Gehrig replied, "It's a pretty big shadow...As long as I was following Ruth to the plate, I could have stood on my head, and no one could have known the difference." And that "Iron Horse" nickname didn't come easy. In an X-ray of Gehrig's hands late in his career, doctors spotted 17 different fractures that healed while Gehrig was playing in 2,130 consecutive games.

The Iron Horse On June 2, 1925, Yankees manager Miller Huggins replaced slumping first baseman Wally Pipp in the lineup with the 21-year-old Lou Gehrig, who would go on to play the next 2,130 games in a row. Then, on May 2, 1939, Gehrig, as the Yankee captain, handed the lineup card to umpires before the game. And for the first time in 14 years, his name was not on it. In 1941 Gehrig would eventually succumb to the disease that now bears his name—exactly 16 years to the day that he replaced Wally Pipp on June 2.

When I started my professional career, Bill "Moose" Skowron was the Yankees first baseman. Moose had gone to Purdue on a football scholarship. But that's not how he got his nickname. Instead it came from a bad haircut he got as a kid. His friends started calling him "Mussolini" after the bald Italian dictator. That got shortened to "Moose," and it stuck the rest of his days.

Moose had a high-pitched voice, and after I found out he was a lethal high ball hitter, I began to throw him the slowest curveballs I could throw. He would beat them into the ground and as he was running down the first-base line he would scream at me, "How can a guy so big throw so slow? Throw the ball like a man!" It was all to try and get me to throw him a fastball. I never took the bait. Moose continued to get a diet of slow curves and he went right on screaming at me.

Moose was traded to the Dodgers after the 1962 season to make room for Joe Pepitone, who became a fixture at first through most of the '60s. The Brooklyn-born Pepitone was beloved in the Bronx. And while he won three Gold Gloves covering first, he is perhaps most known for an error in the 1963 World Series. The Yanks had lost the first three games and were in sunny L.A. for Game 4. With the game tied 1–1 in the seventh inning, Jim Gilliam of the Dodgers hit a routine grounder to Clete Boyer at third. He threw it to first, and Pepitone lost sight of the ball in the glare coming off of all the white shirts of the men in the stands. Gilliam would go to third on the error and eventually score the series' deciding run. And the best hitter in the series for the Dodgers was none other than the man Pepitone replaced at first, Skowron.

When I came to play for the Yankees in 1979, the first baseman was Chris Chambliss. He'd come over from Cleveland in a trade back in April of '74. Chris was named Rookie of the Year with the Cleveand Indians in 1971 and he won a Gold Glove with the Yankees in 1978. By then the team was calling him "the Snatcher" because if a throw was coming in low, he would just "snatch" it out of the dirt in one big swoop. He definitely saved plenty of E4s, E5s, and E6s with that glove. But Chris was better known by Yankee fans for his bat—and for one swing in particular.

It came in the 1976 American League Championship Series against the Kansas City Royals. The Yankees were finishing their first season in the remodeled Yankee Stadium. This was their first playoff series at home in 12 years. The teams split the first four games, so it all came down to a chilly night on Thursday, October 14th—for a spot in the World Series. The Yanks had a 6–3 lead going into the eighth inning when George Brett got ahold of a pitch from Grant Jackson and put it over the short wall in right to tie the score.

The bottom of the eighth and top of the ninth were scoreless. So it came down to the bottom of the ninth. Royals reliever Mark Littell took the mound to face the No. 4, 5, and 6 hitters for the Yankees, starting with Chambliss. Chris was having a great season, making the All-Star team for the only time in his career. And he was having a heck of a game that night with a single, a double, a sacrifice fly, two runs scored, and a stolen base. At 11:43 PM Chambliss dug in, and Littell threw his first pitch. Phil Rizzuto on WPIX took it from there.

He hits one deep to right center, that ball is...outta here! The Yankees win the pennant! Holy cow, Chris Chambliss on one swing! And the Yankees win the American League pennant. Unbelievable, what a finish! As dramatic a finish as you'd ever want to see.

The drama actually continued even after the swing. After enduring a 12-year postseason drought, Yankees fans had a lot of pent-up energy. It boiled over once Chambliss' hit landed in the right-field seats. Thousands of fans stormed the field. Many ran out to congratulate Chambliss for delivering them to the World Series. Others looked like they were there to grab Chris' batting helmet right off his head for a souvenir. Chambliss was actually knocked over between second and third by overexuberant fans. It was pretty chaotic out there, and nothing you are prepared to face—no matter how long you've been playing baseball. "He is being mobbed by the fans," said Scooter as he watched. "And this field will never be the same. The safest place to be is up here in the booth!" Interestingly enough, Reggie Jackson was also up in the booth at that time. He was about to become a free agent of the Oakland A's, whose season was over. He was working the game for ABC Sports and was in the booth with Keith Jackson and Howard Cosell when Chambliss made contact.

By the time Chambliss rounded third base, the area around home plate was an absolute madhouse. Chris had to fight his way through the swarming fans. If you watch it now, he almost disappears in the mayhem as he fights his way to the safety of the dugout.

Later, back in the clubhouse with his celebrating teammates, Chambliss was approached by third baseman Graig Nettles. "Chris, did you touch home plate? It's not an official home run until you do." Chris said, "I couldn't. I couldn't even see it. There were just too many people there." The Royals manager at the time was Whitey Herzog, and if anyone knew all the ins and outs of the rule book, it was Whitey. The last thing the Yankees needed was to lose this dramatic victory on a technicality. So Chris went back out onto the field to step on home plate—this time with an escort for his protection. They cleared the way and got Chris to home plate…*only it wasn't there.* Some fan had taken it. So Chris stepped where home plate had been to complete the most dramatic hit of his career. And you have to figure that somewhere in the greater metropolitan area, in some die-hard Yankees fan's den, there sits the home plate from that amazing game. But it is missing a footprint from one Carroll Christopher Chambliss.

That home run announced to the world that the Yankees were back. And while they would lose the World Series to the Cincinnati Reds in four games, they stayed at the center of the baseball world for the next two years, returning to those championship glory days that were so familiar in the Bronx. From my perspective, Chris was a very deserving yet curious choice to be the guy behind this high-profile moment. Chris was always very low-key and soft-spoken. There was nothing flamboyant about him. A real top-quality guy, as well as a good player and teammate, he was not the guy you would expect to be the center of attention. But then, that's one of the great things about baseball; anyone who steps up to the plate with the game on the line can become a hero with one swing of the bat. And the Yankees have a lot of those types of heroes.

One Swing Can Change Everything
Besides punctuating the change in the Yankees' fortunes, the Chambliss home run also changed the game of baseball. After Chris' difficulty in trying to touch home, Major League Baseball amended rule 4.09 to add an exception. Rule 4.09(b) now reads in part, "An exception will be if fans rush onto the field and physically prevent the runner from touching home plate or the batter from touching first base. In such cases, the umpires shall award the runner the base because of the obstruction by the fans." The addition is called "The Chris Chambliss Rule."

Chris also played a part in the Yankees' success in the late '90s. He was the team's hitting coach for the four World Series titles won from 1996 to 2000, giving Chambliss six championships in pinstripes. He and

Willie Randolph are the only Yankees to play major roles in the glory years of both the 1970s and 1990s. Chambliss' long run of success is not surprising when you hear his philosophy. When it comes to baseball, Chris said, "If you are not having fun, you miss the point of everything."

The "who" on first during the championship years of the late '90s was Tino Martinez. Tino grew up in West Tampa, Florida, not far from where fellow Yankee Lou Piniella had his roots. In fact their families knew each other. Tino was drafted by the Mariners and played for Piniella in Seattle. And he helped Seattle win that famous Game 5 of the American League Division Series in '95. That game, of course, was the last in Don Mattingly's great career as a player. A few months later, Tino was in New York trying to fill the shoes of Donnie Baseball.

Like a lot of the players who get traded to the Yankees, Tino started off slowly. Playing in New York is unlike playing anywhere else. There is just so much hype, and everything you do is under a media microscope. So it is not easy to step into pinstripes and be great. And in Tino's case, replacing a legend only made it that much harder. So he went through the tough times early in the year, trying too hard. But eventually he found his groove. Tino played in the Bronx from 1996 through 2001, going to the World Series every year but '97 and winning it all on four of his five trips.

Tino became one of the veteran leaders. And after Mattingly, I would pick Tino as the best modern Yankees first baseman. He was really good at making that difficult 3-6-3 double play. That's when the first baseman fields it, throws to the shortstop covering second, and then has to beat the runner back to his bag to complete the play. Because he was right-handed, Tino would make that sort of reverse pivot and get off a good throw. He did that as well as anybody.

Tino played in two All-Star Games—in '95 and '97. The latter year was also the season he earned Silver Slugger honors and won the Home Run Derby. But I really think there were a couple years there that Tino deserved a Gold Glove. He didn't get one, but he deserved one at first base. Off the field, he was a terrific guy, part of that Yankees team in the late '90s that was full of not only the good players on the field, but also first-class personalities off of it, which I think added to the value of that team.

One great example of Tino exhibiting true class came after a gut-wrenching defeat. It was Game 7 of the 2001 World Series against the Arizona Diamondbacks. Luis Gonzalez's hit off of Mariano Rivera barely cleared the infield, but it was enough to plate Jay Bell and give the Diamondbacks their first title. The Gonzalez hit also ended New York's hope for four straight World Series titles. But probably the tougher pill for the Yankees to swallow was losing that championship for New York. This series started only seven weeks after the attacks on the World Trade Center, and you could tell that this team really wanted to win this one for their city. But it was not meant to be. For Tino it was a bittersweet moment because the man who won the game for Arizona—Gonzalez—was one of his best friends. They had played little league together in West Tampa and were the leaders of their high school baseball team. When Gonzalez finally got home that night and checked his answering machine chock full of congratulatory messages, the very first one was from Tino.

After the 2001 season, the Yankees signed Jason Giambi from Oakland, and Tino went off to play in St. Louis for a couple of seasons. Thanks to interleague play in 2003, Tino returned to Yankee Stadium. Like most players who have made a name for themselves with one team and return with another, Tino wasn't sure of the reception he would get. He didn't have to wait long to find out. When he came up to bat, he was given a long and loud standing ovation from Yankees fans. Sure, Tino was there wearing Cardinals red, but he had been such a big part of the Yankees' recent success that the faithful couldn't let this opportunity go by without saying thanks. The gesture moved Tino to tears. In the second game of the series, Tino hit a home run off of his old teammate Andy Pettitte and got cheered. And then in the ultimate sign of respect, the fans cheered for a curtain call—from an opposing player! It is a rare honor for a visiting team member to be asked to tip his hat to the fans in the Bronx, but it was an honor that Martinez more than deserved.

After a short stint with the Tampa Bay Rays in '04 (where he was reunited with old friend, Sweet Lou), Tino was back in the Bronx in 2005. He had definitely lost a step, but he still had his moments like when he hit at least one home run in five straight games in May. Then, after failing to hit one out for a sixth straight game, he hit one out in the next game and two in the game after giving him eight dingers in eight games. At the end of the season, Tino wanted to hang 'em up. He wanted to try his hand at broadcasting and took a job with ESPN. In 2010 he replaced David Cone on the YES Network. And in 2013 he was back in uniform as a hitting coach for the Miami Marlins. But in June of 2014, Tino returned to New York as the Yankees honored him with a plaque in Monument Park.

So what about the man who replaced Tino at first in 2002? Giambi was a free-spirited California dude who played hard and loved to have fun. He was the American League MVP in 2000 for the A's. But after signing a $120 million contract, like most newcomers to New York, he had a difficult time at the plate and experienced the expected boos from the Yankees faithful early on. But on a rainy night in May, all of that changed. The Yanks were playing the Minnesota Twins, and it was far from a pitching duel. Bernie Williams hit a solo shot in the bottom of the ninth inning to tie the game at nine and force extra innings. But in the top of the 14th, New York gave up three runs, and things were not looking good for the Yankees or their fans, who had braved the weather to stick around until the end.

The Yankees rallied and loaded the bases with one out when Giambi stepped to the plate for the eighth time that game. A single would get the Yankees back in the game. Instead, Giambi hit the first pitch he saw from Mike Trombley and parked it in the right-field bleachers for a walk-off grand slam. With a single swing of the bat, the Yankees went from 12–9 down to 13–12 winners. The relief in the organization was palpable. Joe Torre said after the game, "That's what everybody has been waiting for since we signed him." But my announcing partner Michael Kay really put his finger on it when he said, "Now Jason Giambi is officially a Yankee." It seems every player who wears the pinstripes has to do something memorable before they are accepted into the family. And this was pretty memorable. The last Yankees player to hit a walk-off grand slam to win a game with New York down three runs was Babe Ruth in 1925—not bad company to keep for Jason.

Who Is on First? In 1997 Jason Giambi replaced Mark McGwire as Oakland's first baseman when McGwire was traded to St. Louis. In 2002 Gimabi replaced Tino Martinez at first in the Bronx. As for Tino, after taking over for Don Mattingly in New York, he goes to St. Louis and replaces another larger than life first baseman...McGwire.

If you start a conversation about Yankees first basemen with Gehrig, then you should probably end it with Mattingly. Don had a lot of nicknames. "The Hit Man" was one; "Don Battingly" was another. But most know him still as "Donnie Baseball." Mattingly made his Yankees debut in 1982, but his breakout season came in '84. That's when Don was battling his teammate Dave Winfield for the American League batting title. Don was .002 points behind Winfield on the final game of the season. Dave went 1-for-4, and Don went 4-for-5 to edge out Winfield .343 to .340. Even early on you could tell Mattingly didn't shy away from pressure. (Oh, if only he had more chances in the postseason.) As good as he was in '84, he was even better in '85, taking home the AL MVP as well as the first of his nine Gold Gloves. In '86 he hit 53 doubles, breaking the Yankees record of 52 hit by none other than Gehrig. But in 1987 his back

Don Mattingly crouches in his familiar batting stance in 1987, a year in which he hit .327 with 30 home runs and 115 RBIs.

problems began. How they started has been a topic of debate. Some newspapers reported it was from clubhouse horseplay with pitcher Bob Shirley; both Mattingly and Shirley denied those claims. But what isn't up for debate is that Don's bad back kept him from achieving numbers that his talents were certainly capable of. I think the career of a healthy Mattingly is a cinch for the Hall of Fame. It just didn't last long enough. But he was such a popular guy because of the way he went about his business.

It also didn't help that the Yankees went through some lean years just as Donnie hit the scene. The year before Donnie got there, the Yankees lost the '81 World Series to the Los Angeles Dodgers. They didn't make the postseason again until 1995. And here is where you have to think this guy is really snake bit. In 1994 the Yankees have the best record in the American League, but the players' work stoppage led to the postseason being canceled. And yet, through it all, good times and bad, Donnie was a fan favorite.

During one Old Timers' Day, Michael Kay was announcing all the Yankees in attendance. There was a tradition that, as they got down to the last few names on the list, they would be read in order of significance to the Yankees with the biggest names saved for last. For a long time, that was Joe DiMaggio. And then that person became Yogi. And then one day, because of Scooter's failing health, they had him introduced last. But for a while, Whitey Ford, Scooter, and Yogi would be the final few, and they would usually be preceded by Reggie Jackson. Now, Reggie could have a little issue with his ego, but he never had a problem with those three legends following him.

But on this one Old Timers' Day, Michael introduces Reggie, then Mattingly, and *then* the three real old timers. The day after, Reggie kind of threw his hands up to Michael and said, "You introduced me before Mattingly? Why?" And Michael had to say, quite frankly: "Yeah, because he is a more popular player than you, Reggie." Even though Reggie had the Mr. October reputation and all of his accomplishments in the World Series, Don was Donnie Baseball and the fan favorite in New York.

Don's career after his playing days hasn't hurt his standing with Yankees fans. He coached alongside Joe Torre in New York from 2004 to 2007 and then followed him to L.A. to work with the Dodgers. When Joe retired in 2011, Don took over. This is all a surprise to me because Don was one of those guys I never thought would have any interest in managing. Most super successful players are focused on their own careers so much that they really don't pay as close attention to the details of the game like the guys sitting on the bench most of the time. Donnie had a lot of ideas as a hitting coach. That was his strength, and I think he watched Torre and others he played for enough that he was motivated to be a manager, and he is obviously doing well at it with the Dodgers.

But no matter what success he achieves with the Dodgers, Mattingly will forever be a Yankee. His No. 23 will never be seen again in pinstripes. It was retired at a ceremony at Yankee Stadium on August 31, 1997. A misty-eyed Mattingly stood on the field and thanked Yankees fans for their years of support. A plaque in Monument Park was also dedicated in his honor. There, fans, who never saw him play, can get an idea of the man and what he meant for all those years to the Yankees family. It reads in part, "A humble man of grace and dignity, a captain who led by example...dedicated to the pursuit of excellence. A Yankee forever."

The Hot Corner

In the sport of cricket, there is a position called "silly mid on." It's called "silly" because the poor chap who plays it must get close to the batter on the side that he would pull the ball. He is there to catch weak tips or deflections. But if the batter gets ahold of one and really drives it, Mr. Silly Mid On will have very little time to defend himself, let alone make the play.

In baseball, we don't put anyone in a "silly" position, but the player closest to that would have to be the third baseman. The balls coming at him from right-handed pull hitters are often coming in "hot" or really fast. That, along with the long throw to first, are the main challenges of playing third. Over the course of my career, I've been fortunate to see some outstanding third basemen in the Bronx. But some of them would be found guilty of doing or saying things that could definitely be considered silly.

When I broke into the majors, third base in the Bronx was in the skilled hands of Clete Boyer. Clete was never much of a hitter, but he more than made up for it on the field. He played for the Bombers from 1959–66 and won two titles in '61 and '62. For several years in the early '60s, Boyer led the league in putouts, assists, and double plays by a third baseman—outperforming even the great Brooks Robinson. And yet it was Robinson who won the Gold Glove each time. Clete would finally win his in 1969 with the Atlanta Braves.

An interesting note about Clete: he was one of seven brothers who all played professional baseball, and three of the boys reached the majors. Besides Clete, his brothers Cloyd and Ken both played for the Cardinals. Cloyd was a pitcher while Ken played third. And in 1964 Clete and Ken made history, becoming the first brothers on opposing teams to both hit a home run in a World Series game. Ken hit his off of New York's Steve Hamilton and nodded to his brother as he rounded third base. Later, Clete took the great Bob Gibson out of the yard and returned the nod to his brother as he headed for home. But it would be Ken who would get the last laugh. His Cards won the World Series in seven games.

The best Yankee third baseman of all time, in my opinion, is Graig Nettles and not just because I got to play alongside him on two different teams. On and off the field, he was great to be around. I first met Graig when he came up with the Twins in 1967. Back in those days, if you were a September call-up, it was often hard to find a place in your new home city. So veteran players would take the rookies into their homes for the rest of the season. Graig and his wife, Ginger, ended up living with my family in Minnesota for the last month of the '67 season. They also brought along their dog "Ofer," as in "I went 0-for-5 yesterday." How do you not like a guy who names his dog Ofer?

I remember spring training in 1968 with the Twins. We played at Tinker Field in Orlando, Florida. And like a lot of spring training fields in those days, Tinker was pretty substandard. A lot of rocks and bumps made it difficult to play on that infield, particularly when the weather turned hot. They didn't maintain it well, so those rutty bumps became the size of freeways before you knew it. Graig made a few errors on this moonscape of an infield. It just so happened that Calvin Griffith, the owner and general manager of the Twins, was there watching. His reaction was: "We gotta get that kid in the outfield." So the Twins put Graig in the outfield, thinking he couldn't play third base. And that perception stayed with management until December of 1969 when they engineered a trade, and Nettles was off to Cleveland. Indians manager Alvin Dark had penciled Nettles in as his third baseman, calling all that talk that he couldn't play third "unfounded rumors." Nettles was always grateful for Dark's confidence in him and he repaid it by becoming one heck of a third baseman for the Indians.

Nettles would join the Yankees in 1973 as part of a six-player trade with Cleveland. For the next 10 seasons, Graig held down the hot corner in the Bronx. A six-time All-Star, he collected two Gold Gloves and an American League home run crown, proving his value both at the plate and in the field. He was a cornerstone of the championship teams, winning back-to-back titles against the Dodgers in '77 and '78. His 319 home runs are still the most by a third baseman in the AL (though Adrian Beltre and Miguel Cabrera are closing in on Graig's home run record). And in the long history of the franchise, Nettles is one of only 11 players to hold the title of Yankees captain. His performance in the 1981 ALCS against the Oakland A's, where he hit .500, earned him

MVP honors. But then in the World Series that year, things would fall apart. The Yankees won the first two games at Yankee Stadium. But in Game 2, Nettles dove for a ball and broke his thumb. He did not play the three games in Los Angeles—all won by the Dodgers. Nettles returned for Game 6, but this time the Dodgers would not be denied, and they took the series in six games. It would be 15 years after Nettles broke his thumb before the Yankees would win another World Series game.

In the clubhouse and on the bus, Graig was always very deadpanned and always seemed to have a cool one-liner ready to go for any situation. His famous line about playing in New York during the Bronx Zoo years was: "When I was a little boy, I wanted to be a baseball player and join the circus. With the Yankees I have accomplished both." In 1977 Sparky Lyle became the first reliever to win a Cy Young. Then during the offseason, the Yankees signed Goose Gossage as a free agent. Goose had a great start in '78, and all of a sudden, Lyle was expendable. Graig's take on the situation said it all. According to Sparky in his famous book, *The Bronx Zoo*, Nettles said Lyle went, "from Cy Young to Sayonara." One time the Yankees had a series of base-running mistakes. Those in the media started to wonder if the Yankees needed new first and third-base coaches. Graig's response? "What the Yankees need is a second-base coach." Graig often turned his wicked sense of humor on himself as well. Once while breaking in a new glove he wrote "E-5"—the box score notation for an error by the third baseman—on its side.

Graig may have been quick with a joke, but he was also quick to defend his teammates if needed. In May of 1976, the Yanks were playing the hated Red Sox, and Lou Piniella crashed into Boston catcher Carlton Fisk at home. Fisk took exception. Punches were thrown, and benches cleared. Nettles was on second base at the time and ended up charging Red Sox pitcher Bill Lee and tackling him from behind. Lee ended up hurting his shoulder and was put on the disabled list for six weeks. He vowed when he came back that he'd "drill Nettles." Graig later said the injury to Lee was an accident that happened at the bottom of a pile of players. He even said the oft-quoted Lee should be happy. "I hurt his shoulder," Graig said. "He earns his living with his mouth. It would've been worse if I had broken his jaw, and it had to be wired shut for a few days." He could really keep the clubhouse loose.

In addition to being a great player, he was a good friend throughout all these years. He was a fun teammate to have—as a young player and then as a veteran and a really important part of that Yankees team. He ranks up there with Boyer in how they didn't have great foot speed, but they could backhand the ball and throw a laser to first. Graig was also a prototypical corner player in that he didn't hit for a high average, but he hit a lot of home runs. And then there's all of those outstanding plays he made behind third base. It's hard to decide what to remember Graig for the most—his bat, his glove, or his tongue. If they kept stats on all three, he'd be in the Hall of Fame for sure. In the winter of 1984, the Yankees picked up Toby Harrah from the Indians, intending to platoon him along with Graig at third in the upcoming season. Nettles made it clear he wasn't happy with that and on March 30th he was traded to his hometown San Diego Padres for pitcher Dennis Rasmussen and the old "player to be named later." Graig would play for the Braves and Montreal Expos as well before retiring in 1988.

When Nettles left the Yankees, the hot corner in the Bronx became a bit of a revolving door. In the next 21 years, at least 46 players tried their hand at third for the Bombers. A few of them stuck around long enough to make some impressions. One of the first was Yogi's son, Dale Berra. He was an infielder who saw time at third in '85 and '86. Yogi began the '85 season as the manager of the Yankees. That made Dale the first son to play for his father since Connie Mack's son, Earle, played for the Philadelphia A's in 1914. Unfortunately, when Yogi was fired just 16 games into the season, Dale went from a starter to a backup role under Billy Martin. Dale had the same funny, dry sense of humor as his father. I'll never forget our time as spring teammates in 1984 when I tried out with the Pittsburgh Pirates. It was pouring down rain, and as we sat in the dugout, "Yogi," as we called Dale, stood outside in a downpour. Willie Stargell asked him why he was out in the rain. Dale's response: "It's a dry rain."

While I was working for MSG Network in 1996, I inadvertently got into a controversial situation with a pair of Yankees third basemen. At the time backup catcher Jim Leyritz and Wade Boggs were splitting time playing third. Boggs, of course, made a name for himself in Boston, playing 11 seasons for the Red Sox and winning five AL batting titles with them. By the time he joined the Yankees in 1993, he was still swinging a mean bat and was well on his way to 3,000 hits. And he had improved his defense, winning Gold Gloves in '94 and '95. But by the next season, his 15th in the league, he was beginning to show some wear and tear.

So the Yankees made a deal to acquire Charlie Hayes, a slick fielding third baseman from Pittsburgh. Charlie had played for the Yankees in '92 before spending the next few seasons bouncing around the National League. But his return to New York wasn't seen by everyone in the clubhouse as a good thing. Upon hearing the news, Leyritz said something like, "I don't know why they got Charlie Hayes. Me and Boggs can handle third quite nicely." Boggs, who was closing in on a batting milestone said, "Guess I'll have to go elsewhere to get my 3,000 hits." So those comments were out there in the press, and both struck me as being a little self-centered. I'm sure they didn't mean it to come off that way, but to my ear, that's how it sounded. When I was asked what I thought about the whole thing, I did what I always did on air: I spoke my mind. I said, "The Yankees acquiring Charlie Hayes will give them some stability at third base. I think that's good move for the team. And the quotes from Leyritz and Boggs come off as being a little selfish to me."

Back then, we had a sponsored element, a Budweiser Quote of the Day. And so the next day, the Quote of the Day was Leyritz's quote about him and Boggs being able to handle third without Hayes. My response to that was plain and simple: "If Jim Leyritz thinks he can play third base as well as Charlie Hayes, he's never seen Charlie play." I was paid to call 'em like I saw 'em, and that's how I saw this one. The next day the Yankees are playing in Oakland when Leyritz comes up to me in the clubhouse and says, "I want to talk to you." Leyritz was not shy and never short on confidence. When he was hitting a .189, he continued to think and act like he was a .300 hitter. So he pulls me aside and said: "My dad watched the game last night and he said you ripped me."

"I did? What did I say?"

"You said I couldn't play third base."

"Hold on," I said. "Want to look at the tape? I said, 'If you think *you* can play third base as well as Charlie Hayes, you've never seen Charlie play.' That's what I said. And quite frankly, I don't think you can play third as well as Hayes. Do you?"

Jim had no response to that and he offered no apology. So I went on about my business getting ready to call the game. The next day it was Boggs' turn to call me over.

"I heard what you said about me being selfish," he said, "about talking about wanting 3,000 hits while I'm playing on a team with a chance to go to the World Series."

"That's right."

"Well," Boggs said, "you were right. I didn't want it to come out that way, but I could see how you could interpret it as selfish."

I definitely appreciated that. Boggs realized I'm not there to try and embarrass the players. I'm there to report on them. And if they put something out there that that is questionable or not very smart, that's what I report. Of course, that also means that I can help set the record straight if it needs straightening. "Well, Wade," I said, "Tell me how you *did* want it to come out, and I'll clean it up for you."

So he did. And when I got on the air, I said, "I talked to Wade

Boggs about what he said about Hayes' arrival, and he admitted that it came out of frustration. The first thing he thought of was the 3,000 hits and how not getting a chance to play would impact that. But that was in the heat of the moment. He definitely understands that adding Charlie is better for the team and he is good with that."

In the end things all worked out. Hayes, Boggs, and Leyritz all helped the Yankees reach the postseason and win their first championship in 18 years. Boggs even celebrated by jumping on the back of an NYPD horse and riding around the field at Yankee Stadium in celebration. In 1998 Boggs left for Tampa Bay, where he grew up, and joined the Devil Rays for their inaugural season. In fact he hit the first home run in Devil Rays history. And while it took a few more years, Wade got his 3,000th hit on August 7th, 1999.

Reaching 3,000 with a Bang! Over his 18-year career in the majors, Wade Boggs was known as a tough out, not as a long ball hitter. His .328 career batting average contained a lot of singles slapped through holes and only 118 career homers. Boggs once told *The New York Times*, "I love to hit home runs. I was a home run hitter in high school, but then something happened. The parks just got bigger." But when he got his 3,000th hit that August night in Tampa, it came in the form of a home run. Boggs even kissed home plate after circling the bases.

Of the 28 players in the 3,000 hits club, only two hit one out for their 3,000th hit. The other was Derek Jeter in 2011.

I may have had a small hand in one of the most successful Yankee third basemen in recent memory coming to the Bronx. Scott Brosius was the starting third baseman for the A's for most of the early '90s. He had a solid year in '96 but declined in '97. I knew Oakland had Eric

Scott Brosius celebrates his two-run home run, which tied Game 5 of the 2001 World Series in the bottom of the ninth inning.

Chavez coming up in the minors, and that made Brosius expendable. With that in the back of my mind, I happened to be talking to Yankees GM Bob Watson. The conversation wandered around and settled on Kenny Rogers. Kenny was a left-handed pitcher who just didn't fit in in New York, and the organization was trying to move him. And since the club was also in search of a regular third baseman, I said to Bob, "The A's are going to get rid of Brosius. You know, a perfect trade would be Brosius for Kenny Rogers." I don't know if that started the ball rolling, or if it was just coincidence and the wheels had already been turning, but the next thing you know, that's exactly the trade they made. Rogers was off to the Bay Area, and Brosius was bound for New York.

Brosius' first year in the Bronx was a revelation. He hit .300 and drove in 98 runs to go along with 19 homers. He made the All-Star team for the only time in his career in '98. And when the Yanks reached the World Series that year against the Padres, he really turned it on, hitting .471 with six RBIs. His two homers in Game 3 that gave New York a 3–0 series lead that probably sealed his World Series MVP honors. His numbers would drop the next few years but not his stature in the eyes of the Yankees faithful. There's something about his blue-collar approach to the game that really hit home with the fans. His teammates loved him, too. Scott was a gamer.

The Yankees won the pennant every year Brosius was in New York, not to mention three championships. He had one of the stronger throwing arms of any infielder and he grabbed a Gold Glove in 1999 for good measure. But Scott's biggest moment on the big stage came in 2001. With the World Series tied 2–2 and the Yankees down to their last out in Game 5, Brosius hit a two-run shot off of Byung-Hyun Kim to tie the game in the bottom of the ninth, mirroring Tino Martinez's effort the night before in Game 4. In the history of the World Series, a team had never hit a two-out, two-run home run in the bottom of the ninth to tie a game, and here the Yankees did it on back-to-back nights! Unfortunately, the magic didn't hold that year, and the Yankees lost in seven games. Brosius retired the following offseason.

What I always said about Scott, with no disrespect to Alex Rodriguez, is that if I had to name my best Yankees team during that era in the '90s when they were winning multiple World Series, they were a better team with Brosius at third base than they were with Rodriguez. And Scott is also a top-quality person. He still coaches some baseball out in his native state of Oregon at his alma mater, Linfield College.

After Brosius retired, the Yankees brought in Robin Ventura from the New York Mets. Over at Shea Stadium, Robin became the first player in history to hit a "grand slam single." It came in Game 5 of the '99 National League Championship Series between the Mets and Braves. With the score knotted at 3–3 in the bottom of the 15th inning and the bases loaded, Ventura launched one over the right-center field fence to win the game. But the ecstatic Mets players grabbed Robin and hoisted him on their shoulders before he could circle the bases. The hit was officially scored a single. (I wonder if the umps knew about the Chris Chambliss Rule.)

Humble, self-deprecating, talented beyond belief but not impressed at all with himself, Robin was pleasure to cover, even before he made the big leagues. I had the privilege of covering him when he hit safely in more consecutive games than Joe DiMaggio. Robin went 58 straight games with a hit when he was at Oklahoma State in 1987. He still holds the NCAA Division I record and was in the inaugural class of the College Baseball Hall of Fame. Ventura's accomplishments also extend overseas. He, along with fellow Yankees Jim Abbott and Tino Martinez, helped Team USA take home the gold in baseball at the 1988 Olympic Games in Seoul, South Korea. Robin was always very popular and respected by his teammates. His numbers in New York didn't reflect his talent level. A devastating ankle injury he suffered in spring training with the White Sox back in 1997 never healed correctly. It was only after he retired in 2004—and was walking with a cane—that it was discovered his leg muscles were slowly atrophying. Surgery in 2005 corrected the problem, and now as the manager of the White Sox, he can walk out to yell at umpires without any pain in his legs whatsoever.

Another third baseman who looms large in Yankee lore played only a single season in the Bronx. And he is remembered for two plays—one on the diamond and the other on the basketball court. Aaron Boone was a youngster when I was with the Phillies and a teammate of his dad, Bob Boone. When he was a young boy, Aaron was really good at mimicking the stances, swings, and pitching motions of all of us. His brother, Bret, looked more like a future big leaguer than Aaron, but Aaron developed into a very good player. But his claim to fame in the Bronx will always be that one swing he took back in 2003.

Looking back now from 2014, where Boston has won three titles in 10 years, it's a little hard to remember what power the so-called "Curse of the Bambino" held over Red Sox Nation. Before trading Babe Ruth to the Yankees in 1919, the Sox had won five of the first 15 World Series. Since that trade—bupkis. Zip. Zilch. Nada. Nothing. They had come close a few times only to lose in spectacular fashion. They lost in seven games to the Cardinals in '67, to the Reds in '75, and to the Mets in '86. And let's not forget Bucky Dent's home run over the Green Monster in that one-game playoff in '78. It really did seem like the Sox were cursed. Aaron Boone only added to that feeling.

In the bottom of the 11th inning of Game 7 of the 2003 ALCS, knuckleballer Tim Wakefield came in for his second inning of relief. Mariano Rivera had just pitched his third inning, so his tank was all but empty, and the Yankees needed to get something done then and there. Boone hadn't even started the game and he was 1-for-10 against Wakefield. But on the first pitch, he took a big swing and made contact. Once it stayed fair, Boone shot his arms up in the air. His walk-off home run not only won the game, but it also won the series and sent the Red Sox back to Boston empty-handed again. The *New York Daily News* called it the "Curse of the Boonebino." Boston fans simply called him "Aaron [expletive] Boone."

Boone's other contribution was an inadvertent one. In the offseason Aaron tore a ligament in his knee while playing in a pick-up basketball game. That game was a violation of his contract, and the Yankees cut him in late February. Suddenly they were in need of a third baseman. And there was a guy named "A-Rod" out there.

Rodriguez is a once-in-a-lifetime talent. It's as if the baseball gods took all the best skills from the diamond and put them all into a skinny kid from Washington Heights, New York. Over his 20-year career, A-Rod is batting .299 with more than 650 home runs and 2,900 hits. He is a 14-time All-Star with 10 Silver Sluggers, two Gold Gloves, and three AL MVPs. But having a lot of talent at a very young age is a challenge in and of itself. And history is full of stories of people like that, and more often than not, they don't end well.

Milestones On August 4, 2007, eight days after his 32nd birthday, Alex Rodriguez becomes the youngest player to hit 500 home runs when he took Kyle Davies of the Kansas City Royals deep in Yankee Stadium. Exactly three years later, on August 4th, 2010, he becomes the seventh and youngest player in major league history to hit 600. That milestone came at the expense of Shaun Marcum of the Toronto Blue Jays.

Rodriguez was drafted No. 1 overall straight out of Westminster Christian High School by the Seattle Mariners in 1993. He made his major league debut the very next year, becoming only the third 18-year-old shortstop to play in the big leagues in the 20th century. And it didn't take long for him to start turning heads. In 1996 he was a very close second to the Rangers' Juan Gonzalez in MVP voting. Rodriguez, who was 21 at the time, came within three points of becoming the youngest MVP in baseball history. He, along with Randy Johnson and Ken Griffey Jr., made Seattle a perennial postseason team through much of the '90s. He was seen as the future of baseball.

Looking back, the first signs of trouble showed up around 2000 when A-Rod hit the free agency market and signed an eye-popping 10-year, $252 million contract with the Texas Rangers. It wasn't just the richest contract in baseball history. It was at the time the most lucrative contract in sports history. I know Alex was a once-in-a-generation talent, so giving him the biggest contract in baseball was not the problem. The problem was the deal was $63 million more than the second-richest contract in baseball! Although A-Rod lived up to much of the hype on the field, winning his first MVP award in 2003, his monster-sized contract was like a weight around the neck of the Rangers front office, preventing them from signing players they needed to fill gaps in their lineup and rotation. The Rangers never made the playoffs while A-Rod was in Arlington and they also finished last each year. And just about the time the Rangers were coming to the conclusion that they needed to get rid of Alex for the sake of the franchise, Boone was limping off of a basketball court with a torn ACL.

Up until this point, all of A-Rod's records came while he played the position of shortstop. The Yankees, of course, didn't need a shortstop; they had one of the best ever in Derek Jeter. But what if they moved Alex to third? The thought of having a left side of the infield consisting of two (at that time) Hall of Fame first-ballot locks…well, it was just too good to pass up. On February 16, 2004, the Yankees traded Alfonso Soriano and prospect Joaquin Arias to the Rangers for A-Rod and $67 million to help pay his contract. (The Rangers had their choice from several Yankee prospects, including Robinson Cano, but ended up selecting Arias.) Yankees fans at the time loved the move. Not only did they get a player who was putting up the best number of his generation, they also prevented the hated Red Sox from getting him. That December the Red Sox were trying to trade Manny Ramirez to Texas for A-Rod, but the deal ran into issues with the players union. Boone hurt himself in

January, and by February Alex was in pinstripes. For the Yankees faithful, this was a win-win. The *Daily News* called it, "Babe Ruth II."

It seemed like the Yankees were now set for years to come. But what I noticed in Alex's first year in New York was that he was having a difficult time getting hits late in the game with runners on base. I mentioned over the air that his swing was too long, and in the late innings, you are facing pitchers coming out of the bullpen who throw consistently in the high 90s. And Alex just couldn't get to the high fastball with that long swing. Derek on the other hand was hitting well in those situations because he had a shorter, quicker, and more compact swing. I even had our TV crew build a side-by-side comparison to show the two different swings.

Now it was always my normal routine to stand around the cage during batting practice before a game and greet all the players. "Hi, Derek," "Hey, Bernie," "How's it going, Paulie [O'Neill]?" "Hi, Alex." And they'd always say, "Hi, Jim" back. Well, the day after that side-by-side photo, there was no "Hi, Jim" from Alex. He just turned his back on me. I tried again, but my greeting was rejected. But that was fine. There are plenty of players to talk to. I didn't need to talk to Alex. So, the year went on with no replies to my batting cage greetings to Alex.

It wasn't until the next spring when Rick Cerrone—not the catcher, but the Yankees media relations director with the same name—told me Alex would like to meet with me. When we did, Alex apologized for his silence last season. He said he had a lot on his plate during his first year in the Bronx. I accepted Alex's apology. And just so he knew where I was coming from, I said, "I work for the viewer. I'm not the players' PR man. Believe me, my job would be easier than it already is, Alex, if you hit 60 home runs, knocked in 200 runs, and the Yankees won every game. But I am hired to tell people what I see based on my experience as a player, so that's why I said what I said." We were cool from then on.

But A-Rod's first year in New York was a pretty dark one in Yankees history. That was the year the Curse of the Bambino finally came to an end—and for Yankees fans—in the worst way possible. With a three games to none lead in the ALCS, the Bronx Bombers were three outs away from dispatching the Red Sox yet again en route to the World Series. But unlike the year before where Boston imploded, this time around, it was the Yankees. A walk, a stolen base, and a single tied the score. David Ortiz would finish the job in the 12th. The Sox then miraculously ran off the next three games to take the pennant and become the first team in baseball to dig themselves out of an 0–3 hole in a best-of-seven series. As for the Yankees, they were in the history books again—only this time not for something they'd want to remember.

So the first year was rough for both Alex and the Yankees. But in his first four seasons with New York, A-Rod grabbed two more AL MVPs, including in 2007. He followed that with a disastrous handling of his contract negotiations. Alex's agent Scott Boras announced A-Rod was opting out of his contract during Game 4 of the World Series between Boston and the Colorado Rockies. Eventually Alex would sign a new 10-year deal, and this one was for $275 million! That continued A-Rod's reign as the most expensive athlete in all of sports.

After the success of the teams in the late '90s, A-Rod's time in New York could not be considered a success until he helped the Yankees win another ring. The 2009 season began auspiciously, however, when A-Rod, after repeated denials, finally said he had used performance-enhancing drugs. He said it happened from 2001 to 2003 when he was with the Rangers. He said it was because he was under intense pressure to perform. My first thought was, *Aren't all players under intense pressure to perform? If A-Rod was under any more pressure, wasn't that of his own doing by going for that giant contract?*

This was also when his hip injury first flared up. He missed spring training and the first month of the season but returned on May 8th and hit the very first pitch he saw for a three-run homer. By mid June, A-Rod had paced the Yanks to first place in the AL East, and despite some ups and downs for both the team and himself, New York made the postseason. Of course, the postseason had not been too friendly to A-Rod. Since Game 4 of the 2004 ALCS, he had gone 0-for-29 with runners in scoring position. That all changed in 2009. A-Rod was lethal at the plate as he helped lead the Yankees to their 27th World Series title, beating the Phillies in six games. A-Rod also earned postseason MVP honors. It seemed that he had finally put himself into that rare air of Yankees legend. But his time on top would be short lived.

The next few years for A-Rod were filled with injuries and accusations. A bad knee, illegal poker games, a hurt thumb, his bad hip, a request by GM Brian Cashman to "shut the f--- up." Teammates and staff were calling him "the Cooler" because teams got "cold" when he was with them and "A-Fraud." It seemed he was always in the news and never for a good reason. Then came the Biogenesis scandal. In August of 2013, Major League Baseball found evidence of A-Rod violating their PED policy and suspended Alex for a whopping 211 games. After an arbitration hearing in January the next year, the suspension was reduced to 162 games—the entire 2014 season. A-Rod and his lawyers originally threatened to sue the league in federal court before accepting the punishment a month later.

Although I am still on good terms with Alex, I am disappointed in some of his behavior during the trial and suspension. I wished he would just say, "I really don't deserve to be on the field now. I'm going to step away from the game until I am allowed back and not be a distraction to my teammates and to the pennant races and the game we love." Instead, he opted to get confrontational, and I thought that hurt him in the eyes of the public and his peers. But all he has to do is show up in the spring of 2015, put on the pinstripes, declare he's ready for action, and he'll get a cool $60 million.

At the time of this writing, A-Rod has become a pathetic figure in sports, a cautionary tale about buying too much of your own hype. There is such a level of narcissism about him that it is hard to find its equal even in the star-driven word of sports. Maybe you can compare him to golfer Greg Norman. I've been around both. They come off so self-centered and so infatuated with their fame that they end up not having any real friends who are their peers. And that only makes the situation worse.

I think Alex's biggest mistake coming to New York was that he actually thought he would become bigger than Derek. He should have had advisors who would have warned him to just lay low and be humble and play ball. In truth, I feel sorry for him, and that in itself is sad because he could have become the greatest player of his era. He certainly had the talent. I always thought Bo Jackson would have been the best of his generation if not for his football injuries. Instead, that mantle, in my opinion, is worn by Ken Griffey, Jr. But it easily could have been A-Rod.

CHAPTER 3
UP THE MIDDLE

Hit a ground ball up the middle of an infield with a man on first and you start one of the most beautiful displays in baseball—the 6-4-3 double play. It requires speed, dexterity, grace, anticipation, and just a little bit of crazy. It's a play that differentiates the shortstop and second baseman from any other duo on the diamond—or in sports for that matter. Besides their own individual defensive responsibilities, short and second must work together with the precision of a dance team—but with the guts of a slot receiver going across the middle in football. Some might say the quarterback and center have a similar simpatico, on-field relationship. But in general they only have to really worry about a snap and shotgun. The variables involved in a double play are astronomical.

History has failed to record whoever first came up with the idea of getting two players out on one batted ball, but I'm sure glad he did. The "pitcher's best friend," as it is often called, has bailed me out of plenty of tight spots over the course of my career. The dangerous ballet of the double play has saved games, series, and even entire seasons. There are plenty of examples where the World Series has turned on a pair of guys turning two. But double plays can go horribly wrong, and more than a few middle infield careers have ended in a heap at second. With that in mind, we take a look at some of the best guys the Yankees have recently played...up the middle. And instead of going by position, we'll check out these guys with the double-play partners.

Richardson and Kubek

Bobby Richardson was the gold standard at second base when I came up to the big leagues. Richardson played 12 seasons—all in New York—racking up seven All-Star invites, five Gold Gloves, three World Series rings, and one World Series MVP. That MVP came in 1960, a year the Yankees lost to the Pittsburgh Pirates on Bill Mazeroski's dramatic Game 7, bottom-of-the-ninth-inning home run. So far Bobby is the only player on the losing team to win a World Series MVP award.

Many a Yankees fan will also remember Richardson snatching a bullet off the bat of Willie McCovey for the final out of the 1962 series. If Bobby didn't make that catch, Willie Mays and Matty Alou more than likely would have scored to give the title to San Francisco. Richardson also had one of those championship turning points, but this time he booted a sure double-play ball in Game 4 of the 1964 series against St. Louis that would have ended the inning. Instead, one batter later, Clete Boyer's brother, Ken, hit a grand slam, and the Cards won the game 4–3 and eventually the series in 7.

I played against Bobby for seven seasons from 1960 to 1966. And I had the impression that he had a really high batting average against me because it always seemed like he was getting a hit when I faced him. I was shocked when I recently looked at our head-to-head record and found he only hit .226 against me during his career. What probably skewed my memory was the fact that Bobby always did the little things at the plate like moving runners over and getting the ball in play. Over his dozen years in the majors, Richardson struck out only 243 times. And late in the game, if the Yankees were tied, he was usually the one who did something—whether it was a bunt or a hit and run—that advanced a runner.

In 1966 Bobby announced he was going to retire. He was only 31 years old, but he was going to hang 'em up. The Yankees decided to honor him for his great years with the team with a Bobby Richardson Day. It fell on a game against my Minnesota Twins, and I was the scheduled starter. By this point it was late in the season, and both the Twins and the Yankees were out of any pennant chase. And while I'm a firm believer in always playing to win the game no matter where you are in the standings, I also believe that if the stars align in such a way that you can help a classy guy like Bobby Richardson shine on his special day, then you should do it—baseball purists be damned.

Well, the stars lined up that day. Bobby came up with nobody on base. So I called my catcher, Earl Battey, out to the mound and said, "Earl, with the bags empty, just tell Bobby to have a nice day." Earl knew what that meant. We were going to pitch him fastballs right down the middle of the plate. Why not give Bobby Richardson a home run on Bobby Richardson Day? So I pitched some of the juiciest pitches I've ever thrown, and Bobby hit four—count 'em *four*—of the nicest little harmless pop-ups you've ever seen. Guess it goes to show how hard it is to hit a baseball. He knew what was coming and still couldn't do anything with them. I ended up getting the win that day. It was a banner year for me, winning 25 games. So those few pitches didn't change the standings or jeopardize my career. But it just goes to show that players will do those goodwill gestures for one another on that rare occasion when they can. I still cross paths with Bobby now and again, and we always have a good laugh at how when I was trying to get him out it always seemed so difficult. And when I was trying to let him hit one, he just popped out.

Richardson's longtime double-play partner and roommate was shortstop Tony Kubek. Like Bobby, Tony played his entire career—nine seasons—in the Bronx, though he missed most of 1962 serving in the Army. And like Bobby he retired young—at 29. Tony's retirement was due to a neck injury that never healed properly. Tony was the Rookie of the Year in 1957 and collected seven pennants and three World Series titles while in pinstripes. What impressed me about his game was he seldom backhanded a ball. He played deep enough in the hole that he could almost always field the ball face on and had a strong enough arm to get the runner. I'm not sure if he could do that if he played today because there is so much more speed in the game now. But it sure worked for him back then.

I also remember in 1960, Tony squared around to bunt on me. The ball ran in and hit him right in the sternum. The worst part for Tony was that it was a strike because he attempted to bunt it. And if you make a play on the ball in the batter's box—swing or bunt—it's a strike, even if it hits you. When we run into each other to this day, he still reminds me that I hit him for a strike.

Tony was on the wrong end of perhaps the worst bad hop grounder in the history of the game. It came in Game 7 of the 1960 World Series against the Pirates. It was the bottom of the eighth inning with the Yankees up 7–4. A routine grounder off the bat of Bill Virdon struck a rock or pebble in the Forbes Field infield and shot up and hit Kubek in the throat. I was once hit in the mouth by a comebacker to the mound off the bat of Bubba Morton of the Detroit Tigers. It knocked two of my teeth out and cracked a third. It also inspired me to improve my fielding. I really have Bubba to thank for helping win 16 Gold Gloves. But I think I'd take losing teeth over getting hit in the throat. I can't think of a worse place to get hit. (Okay, maybe *one* worse place.) Tony was injured so bad on the play that he went straight to the hospital. The Pirates scored five that inning to take a 9–7 lead. The Yankees tied it in the top of the ninth, only to lose it on Mazeroski's heroic shot—the first time the World Series ended on a home run. Five years later doctors weren't able to determine if this was the incident that caused his neck injury. Tony didn't seem to think so. He said he did not have pain in his neck after the bad hop— just a pain in his gut for losing the series. Many think of that 1960 Series as one of the biggest upsets of all time and Game 7 as one of the best in baseball history. Be that as it may, I wouldn't bring up that bad hop to Tony if you see him.

Tony ended up having a major influence on me and my broadcast career. I profited from watching his style, heeding his advice, and receiving his recommendations. And I'm going to go out on a limb and say that pebble did no permanent damage to his throat because now you can find Tony in Cooperstown, not for his work with bat, ball, or glove—but because of his voice. He was honored by the Hall of Fame as a broadcaster in 2008.

Willie and Bucky

During the infamous "Bronx Zoo" years when the only thing more explosive than the Yankees on the field was the team in the clubhouse, the middle of the field was held down by two really solid guys: Willie Randolph and Bucky Dent.

Willie came up with the Pirates in 1975, but after only one season, he was traded to the Yankees, along with Ken Brett and Dock Ellis for George "Doc" Medich, who was a real doctor. Randolph was a rock at second base. He just fit in so nicely on those '77, '78 championship teams. With so many egos in the locker room, the team needed guys like Willie who could get the job done without needing to see his name in the papers. He was not flashy—just extremely effective, an everyday player who could handle the bat and hit the ball to right field. Willie also had a tremendous eye and led the league in walks in 1980. He was good in the field and went to six All-Star Games, though he never won a Gold Glove. Unfortunately for Willie, those usually went to Frank White of the Kansas City Royals or Lou Whitaker of the Tigers during Randolph's prime. But Willie could certainly turn a double play. Just ask any of the 1,547 pairs he doubled up over the course of his career. Willie still ranks third on the all-time list at turning two.

If he got scouted today, Randolph would be in a very interesting category. I don't want to compare him to Pete Rose, but he is a similar type of player. Scouts would say, "Well, he doesn't have a lot of power. He has some speed but not a lot of it. He doesn't have a great arm. But at the end of the day, he's just a great baseball player." And that's what Willie Randolph was. Willie ended his playing days in Queens with the New York Mets in '92. Two years later he was back in the Bronx as a coach for manager Buck Showalter. When Buck was fired and Joe Torre came in, Randolph stayed and became a fixture on Joe's staff all the way through to 2004. He got his first-ever managing job back with the Mets in '05. In 2006 he led the Mets to their first division title in 18 years and came within a game of reaching the World Series. Then, in 2007 the bottom dropped out. In one of the worst collapses in league history, holding a seven-game lead with 17 to play, the Mets went 5–12 and lost the division to the Philadelphia Phillies. The next year Willie was fired in June, but I feel he really got a raw deal. He had a contingent of players that, I think, kind of banded together and made life very difficult for him until the Mets finally let him go. But through it all, Willie has remained the classy guy I always knew, and I am happy to call him a good friend.

Willie's partner in crime in the Bronx Zoo was Russell Earl "Bucky" Dent. Bucky and I played together in Chicago. He was just what you call a lunch pail, everyday, do-your-job shortstop. In 1977 the White Sox traded him to New York for outfielder Oscar Gamble and pitcher LaMarr Hoyt. Bucky's claim to fame of course is the home run he hit in 1978 in the one-game playoff against the Boston Red Sox. I don't know if anyone could have predicted that one, considering Bucky only hit 40 homers during his entire 12-year playing career. Both teams had ended the season with 99 wins. The Sox had had a commanding 14-game lead in July—only to be caught and passed by the Yankees near the end of the season. Then it was the Red Sox, who had to win down the stretch to force the playoff. It was a very exciting season that deserved an exciting finish.

The Yankees were down 2–0 in the seventh inning. Red Sox pitcher Mike Torrez had only given up two hits. But the Yankees put runners on first and second with Dent coming to the plate. Manager Bob Lemon wanted to pinch hit for Bucky, but because of injuries and moves he already made, there was nobody available. So Dent stepped up to the plate and fouled the second pitch off of his left ankle. He usually wore a guard on it, but he didn't this time and went down in a heap. Having no other options, I'm sure Coach Lem was quietly urging him to get up. After Bucky walked it off, he realized his bat was cracked. So Mickey Rivers gave the batboy one of his. While holding Rivers' bat, Dent steps back in, chokes up on the bat like he always did, and waited for Torrez's next pitch. It hung slightly, and Bucky swung for all he's worth. In reality it was just a little fly ball to left field, almost like Bobby Thomson's shot back at the Polo Grounds. But Dent's hit cleared the famous Green Monster. Not by much, mind you, but it did. Years later, Fenway Park groundskeeper Dave Mellor told *The Boston Globe* about the marks left by baseballs in the Green Monster. They call them "dimples" instead of dents because of Bucky F------ Dent.

What made Bucky famous wasn't so much his swing as where he did it. If that game was played in any other stadium in America beside Fenway, Bucky isn't a hero. But it was and it gave New York a 3–2 lead. The Yankees hung on to win 5–4 and gut their New England rivals once again. Buck batted over .400 in the series that year, claiming MVP honors as he led the Yankees past the Los Angeles Dodgers for back-to-back titles.

Bucky played another four seasons in New York before being traded to the Texas Rangers for Lee Mazzilli. Dent was back in the Bronx briefly in '84 but never played a game before retiring with the Royals that year. He went on to coach and manage in the Yankees farm system, eventually taking over the big club for parts of the '89 and '90 seasons. Few people remember that George Steinbrenner would fire Bucky 49 games into the season after a loss at, of all places, Fenway Park. But it was the shot in '78 over the Green Monster that put Bucky on the map for the Yankees, as well as earning him a lot of nicknames in Boston—very few, if any, can be repeated in polite company.

Derek and the Dominos

Since Derek Jeter's arrival in the Bronx nearly 20 years ago, the Yankees have played many second basemen alongside him. A couple of talented shortstops even had to reinvent themselves elsewhere on the diamond—A-Rod at third; Alfonso Soriano at third, then second, then the outfield—because Derek had a stranglehold on their preferred position and proved his worth time and time again both in the field and at the plate. Derek has won titles with platoons, journeymen, and All-Stars at second base. There were years where it felt like every time he made that toss to second to start a double play a different guy was covering the bag. So with all due respect to Eric Clapton's short-lived '70s band, the analogy of Derek and the Dominos seems to fit rather nicely. So here's a look at some of the notable names that covered the middle of the field during the Jeter years.

The man holding down the second sack during Derek's rookie year was Mariano Duncan. There are only two Marianos to ever play in the major leagues; Mo Rivera is the other. Both played their part to bring the Yanks their first title in 18 seasons. Duncan was a solid performer. One of his biggest contributions came not with his glove or his bat but with his mouth. It was his battle cry, which caught on and carried the Bombers to the championship: "We play today. We win today." Short, sweet, and oh so true.

Luis Sojo was a real pro and a Davey Concepcion clone. He wore No. 13 like Davey. Like Davey and his predecessors before him—Luis Aparicio and Chico Carrasquel—there was a long line of exceptional shortstops from Venezuela. Sojo was mostly a utility infielder during his time in the Bronx. A role player, Luis came up big in Game 5 of the Subway Series in 2000. His single plated Jorge Posada as well as Scott Brosius on a throwing error in the top of the ninth inning to give the Yankees a 4–2 lead and eventually their 26th title. It was another case of baseball finding a hero where you least expect it.

Chuck Knoblauch was a big time addition to the Yankees in 1998. I knew of Chuck even before he made it to the Twins—back when he was still at Texas A&M. I was doing Twins games back in the late '80s and I ran into Terry Ryan, who was the head of scouting at time. (Now he's the Twins general manager.) Terry said to me, "Well...I just saw our No. 1 draft pick." I knew he'd been down looking at college players, so I said,

"Who, Scott Livingstone?" He was A&M's third baseman and highest ranked player at the time. "Nope," Terry said. "Chuck Knoblauch. He's going to be our second baseman." Chuck played shortstop and center field in college. But Terry was right. Wayne Terwilliger, a veteran major league player, was the Twins' infield coach and he worked tirelessly to convert Chuck to a second baseman. The experiment was a success because Chuck turned out to be a big part of the Twins' 1991 World Series team.

Jump ahead to 1997, and after losing to the Cleveland Indians in the American League Championship Series, Steinbrenner wanted an upgrade at second base and desperately wanted Knoblauch. He ended up sending four players to Minnesota, including two future All-Stars—shortstop Cristian Guzman and pitcher Eric Milton—but George got his man, and the Yankees had a phenomenal season, winning 114 games and sweeping the San Diego Padres in the Fall Classic. But it wasn't long until Knoblauch started showing signs of the dreaded yips. This is the "disease," if you will, that often afflicts golfers when they stand over three-foot puts, start shaking, and can't sink them. Or sometimes you'll see it in catchers when their arms shake because they start thinking about that man on third when they are throwing the ball back to the pitcher and afraid they'll throw it instead into center field (which is exactly what they end up doing). Suddenly, Knoblauch, the '91 American League Rookie of the Year, a four-time All-Star with a Gold Glove, couldn't make a simple throw to first to save his life.

I told Yankees brass that I knew a minor league instructor who helped me with my throwing technique. His name was Al Monchak, but everyone called him Sarge. Sarge was an instructor for the White Sox and Pirates and later the Braves. He even worked with Joe Torre back in Atlanta. Sarge always recommended getting the ball out of the glove and above your head as quickly as possible when fielding a ground ball. As Knoblauch was struggling, I saw Monchak in the press box and asked him if he could help Chuck. "I could help him in a hurry," Sarge said. I passed that on to the Yankees, but it fell on deaf ears. Chuck continued to struggle. But there was one throw he made in 1999 that one teammate really appreciated.

In every bid for a no-hitter or perfect game, there always seems to be a moment where time stops. Bat meets ball, and its trajectory takes it toward open ground. Suddenly, all the air gets sucked out of the stadium. In the next few moments, the play is either made, and a shot at history continues, or it's not, and the game becomes one of the countless late-inning bids for a no-no that was not to be. But it feels like there is that moment every time. Don Larsen's perfect game in the '56 World Series had one. It came in the fifth inning when Gil Hodges laced one deep to left-center field. Mickey Mantle had been playing Hodges to pull the ball and was over in right-center field. Mick had to cover what looked like more than a football field out there in cavernous Yankee Stadium and make a running backhand grab to keep the perfect game going. (Mickey also hit a solo home run in the fourth inning that turned out to be the winning run.)

For David Cone his moment came with one out in the eighth inning of his perfect game bid on July 18th in 1999. The Expos' switch-hitting second baseman Jose Vidro got ahold of one of David's pitches and drove it sharply back up the middle. As it went by Cone, he thought, *That's it. The perfect game is over.* But Cone turned and saw that Knoblauch had gotten a great jump on the ball and, ranging far to his right, backhanded it before it got to the outfield grass. Of course, now came the tricky part because this was right in the middle of his yips. The speedy Vidro did not give Chuck any time to think, and that actually might have been the best thing for him. Chuck planted his foot, wheeled, and fired a strike right into Tino Martinez's mitt to nail Vidro. Four outs later, Cone is in the record books for throwing the 16th perfect game in MLB history.

Unfortunately, that didn't cure Knobby's throwing issues. The final straw for Chuck was having three throwing errors in six innings in a game against the White Sox in June of 2000. He took himself out of that game. Soon after that he was put out in left field—never to return to second base. As painful as it was to watch Chuck and his throwing issues on the field, it was even sadder to hear what happened after he left the game. He's had multiple assault and battery charges levied against him in several domestic disputes. One such charge led the Twins to cancel plans to add him to their Hall of Fame. It reminded me about something that Kirby Puckett once told me. He said Chuck was his only teammate that he did not like or respect. He said it was because of his attitude. I never saw that from my position as a media person, but I sure hope that, unlike his yips, Knobby gets this issue under control.

In the mid-to-late '90s, Soriano was a shortstop climbing the ranks of the Yankees farm system. But pretty soon it became evident with the emergence of Derek as a star that the Yankees had a decision to make on Soriano. Should they move him to third, second, or use him as a chip for a trade? Now, George had always liked Gary Sheffield. He was a power hitter and a good athlete who grew up in the Tampa area. Sheffield came up with the Milwaukee Brewers but then bounced around to the Padres, Marlins (where he won a ring in '97) Dodgers, and Braves. But George never lost track of him and brought his name up a bunch.

So one spring training, I'm doing an exhibition game in Tampa, and rumors are flying around about a trade—a package including Soriano for Sheffield. I think Sheffield was playing for the Dodgers at the time. George is in his private box, listening to the broadcast while watching the game. And Michael Kay and I started discussing those trade rumors. Almost looking over at George who was maybe a hundred feet down from the press box, I said, "Don't make this trade, George. This kid is going to be a star. He is Hank Aaron with speed." I always thought Soriano had those Hank Aaron quick-as-a-whip wrists, and he could just turn on the ball. And Soriano could run. Well, that trade never happened. George finally got Sheffield in free agency in 2003, shortly before

Soriano was traded for another big name player—A-Rod. But I could openly voice my opinions, and George would take in the right spirit. He never really listened to me, but it never created any acrimony with him. As for Soriano, the ball did continue to jump off his bat. The seven-time All-Star is a member of the 40-40 Club, hitting 40 home runs and stealing 40 bases in a single season. He joined Jose Canseco, Barry Bonds, and the man he was traded for—A-Rod—in the exclusive four-member club in 2006 when he was with the Washington Nationals.

Robinson Cano ended up holding down second base the longest during the Jeter years. He played in New York from 2005 until leaving for the Seattle Mariners via free agency at the end of the 2013 season. You could say baseball was in Cano's blood. His dad, originally signed by the Yankees in 1980, had a cup of coffee in the majors, pitching a few games for the Houston Astros in '89. And, of course, the younger Cano was named after the great Jackie Robinson. At one point or another during his time with the organization, Cano was mentioned as possible trade material for A-Rod, Carlos Beltran, and Randy Johnson. Looking back now, it's a good thing for the Yankees that those particular deals never got done. I remember the first time I saw Cano. He was swinging his bat, and I said to my partner, Kenny Singleton, "He looks like Rod Carew with power." Now, to be fair, Rodney showed some power, hitting 14 home runs in '75 and again in '77 with the Twins. He could've been more of a home run hitter if he wanted, but he hit for average. Robinson just had those very loose, relaxed hands. He generated a lot of bat speed, and with that fluid swing, I couldn't help but think of Rod Carew.

Cano had a great start to his career in the Bronx, getting the second most votes behind Huston Street for the 2005 AL Rookie of the Year Award. He'd go on to collect six All-Star invites, two Gold Gloves, and five Silver Slugger Awards. He also helped the Dominican Republic win the 2013 World Baseball Classic while earning MVP honors for the competition. Of course, Yankees fans remember him more for driving in the final run at the old Yankee Stadium and for making the final assist to win the 2009 World Series. Cano made the game look so easy that sometimes fans thought he was loafing and not giving 100 percent effort. Only his teammates know whether that accusation is right or wrong. But he was a very talented player and fun to cover for the few years that I did.

The Legendary Shortstop

The one thing all of these second basemen had in common was that when they looked to their right—they saw a future first-ballot Hall of Famer. As a testament to Jeter's longevity, most don't even remember the starting shortstop before Derek came in and took over was Tony Fernandez, who was really better known for his time turning two for the Toronto Blue Jays.

If you wanted to measure the amount of pressure the Yankees put on Jeter when he came up for a few games in 1995, all you had to do was look at the number on his back. Jeter was assigned the No. 2. That might not have meant much on other clubs, but single digits in the Bronx carried the weight of tremendous expectations. When you looked out toward Monument Park at Yankee Stadium, here's what you saw:

1	3	4	5	7	8	8	9
Martin	Ruth	Gehrig	DiMaggio	Mantle	Berra	Dickey	Maris

Jersey numbers were used by the Yankees in 1929 and were originally the numbers were assigned to players by their place in the batting order. That's why Ruth is 3, and Gehrig is 4. The Yankees have retired nine double-digit numbers as well, but the biggies, the out-and-out legends tended to favor having a single digit on their backs. (The only other missing single digit—No. 6—was also assigned in 1996 to Joe Torre, who proudly wore No. 6 into the Hall of Fame in 2014.) That meant

Shortstop Derek Jeter tips his cap after hitting a single against the Tampa Bay Rays in 2009 to tie Lou Gehrig for the most hits by a Yankees player. *(AP Images)*

the Yankees were expecting this 20-year-old kid from Michigan to fit comfortably in the storied pinstripe history between Battlin' Billy and the Babe. That, my friends, is pressure. Good thing the kid thrived on it.

Derek was taken sixth overall in the 1992 Major League Baseball Draft by the Yankees. For Derek it was a dream come true…he was always a Yankees fan. For five other teams, his exceptional career would become a nightmare, a daily reminder of what they could have had. But how does a kid from Kalamazoo, Michigan, become a Yankees fan in the first place? It all goes back to Derek's maternal grandmother, whom he would visit each summer in northern New Jersey. Dot Connors was a die-hard Yankees fan, even waiting in line hours as a child to see Babe Ruth lying in state when he passed away in 1948. Derek and Grandma Dot would go to games or stay up late into the night to watch them together on TV. She made Derek a Yankees fan for life.

Even after he was drafted, the Yankees still weren't 100 percent sure of what they had. As good as his numbers were, Derek always seemed to be better in person than he was on paper. And early on, not many in the organization saw him in person. Ron Washington—longtime player, coach, and manager who scouted Derek in the minors for the Mets—famously wrote that Jeter was "not no shortstop." Ron knew the kid could hit but thought he'd be better off at third. So there were plenty of questions still floating around at this point. But since the Yankees used their top draft pick on him, they wanted a quick return on their money. So they threw him into the farm system and moved him along quickly, giving him challenge after challenge. As George Steinbrenner said, "Every year you look for Derek Jeter to stumble, and he just doesn't."

Even with Jeter's place in Yankees and baseball lore solidified, a look at Derek's career stats holds a few surprises. Yes, he has more hits than anyone in the pages of the Yankees history books and is the first player in pinstripes to cross the 3,000 hit barrier. But for all of his memorable home runs during his time in the Bronx—and he's had a bunch of them—Derek has never hit more than 24 in a season. For all of the talk about him being the greatest shortstop of his generation and in the discussion for greatest ever, Derek was never voted league MVP and came in second only one time, in 2006. What really makes Derek truly exceptional doesn't always show up on a stat sheet. Besides his considerable talent, he is a born leader, a class act, a tireless worker, a player who flat out makes his teammates better. I guess you could say even his intangibles have intangibles. He is a remarkable player, and I definitely enjoyed getting a chance to watch him day in and day out for the first 11-plus years of his career.

During his first season with the Yankees, a slow ground ball was hit to the third-base side. Derek charged the ball, fielded it with two hands by reaching over his right foot with his glove, and almost in one motion at ground level threw it to first for the out. I was amazed. I said to Don Zimmer, "This kid makes that play look so easy." Zim, who saw as much baseball as Abner Doubleday, responded, "Best I've ever seen at it, pal." (That was Don's favorite expression, adding "pal" to his responses.) I watched Derek make that play time and time again, and whenever I compared it to other shortstops, D.J. was head and shoulders above anyone else at that play.

He got into 15 games with the team in '95 and watched Don Mattingly like a hawk the whole time he was with the club, observing how the Yankees legend carried himself both on and off the field. There was no, "Hey, look at me" in Derek. In the locker room, unless you asked him something, you wouldn't even know he was there. He didn't speak unless spoken to.

In 1996 Derek became the first rookie to start at short for the Yankees since Tom Tresh back near the start of my playing career in 1962. I think a lot of players and coaches were amazed at what they saw that first season. Cone remembered how the kid ran and threw, and David couldn't help but think, *Wow, this kid's got some talent. This kid's got "it." You could tell he wasn't intimidated, and he wanted to play.* Another former Met, Darryl Strawberry had some advice for Derek. Straw, of course, was once the King of New York and didn't handle it all that well. He saw the talent even back in '95 and he'd tell Derek, "You don't have star potential. You have *mega*star potential." But when they were on the bench together, Darryl would use the opportunity to preach patience to Derek.

D.J. would always listen to advice, but he also wasn't shy about giving it if he thought it could help the team. Also playing his first full season in the Bronx in '96 was Mattingly's replacement at first, Tino Martinez, who had a terrible start to his season, really struggling at the plate. And the fans were letting Tino know they weren't happy, which only made Tino grip the bat that much tighter. Then along comes this rookie with barely more experience playing in the Bronx than Tino had, and he started giving him advice. Tino and Derek had some history. When Derek got his first major league hit in 1995, it came in the form of a single in Seattle. As he stood on the bag, Martinez, then the Mariners' first baseman, was the first to say, "Congratulations." Now it was Derek's turn, and he was telling Tino not to worry, that the fans would come around. Derek would say, "Hey, you're playing baseball for the New York Yankees. Just enjoy it." And Tino thought, *You know what? The kid's right.* Tino relaxed and started hitting, and the fans came around to love him.

Paul O'Neill said it was pretty apparent right from the get-go that Derek was going to be a standout leader. Even though he was younger than most of them, the Yankees very quickly became Jeter's team. He just had that air about him. The way he carried himself, the way he ran, the way he approached everything, the way he wore the uniform, the way he communicated with young fans seated in the front row near the on-deck circle. I remember he'd chat with those nearby fans, and guys would think, *What is he doing? Get your head in the game! We need a hit to win this!* But when it was his turn at bat, Derek would excuse himself from the fans, step into the batter's box, flip some concentration switch that only he had, and get that game-winning hit. It was truly remarkable. You never sensed tension in D.J. It was always—*Hey, another day at the ball-park. I'm having fun.* It was a treat for me to see that, day in and day out.

Derek was very familiar with Yankees royalty even as he was surpassing it. In his first five full seasons in pinstripes, Derek had four World Series rings—the same number as Joe DiMaggio. He also outhit the Yankee Clipper over that same span, collecting 996 to Joe D's 970. Of course, Yogi Berra would always kid Derek about not making it to the World Series in '97. Had the Yankees won that one, they would have had a shot at tying Yogi's five straight titles from 1949–53, heading into the 2001 World Series. Derek didn't mind the teasing. He also didn't mind following one of Yogi's cardinal rules: keep it simple. Derek doesn't complicate things. He's not a sabermetrics guy who got into the reams and reams of statistical data. If something wasn't right with his game, D.J. worked on it until it was. Simple. No magic bullet, just hard work. As Reggie Jackson once noted, Derek "didn't lead the league in anything but victories." Jeter also had a very rare and innate quality about him when he was in those clutch situations. You could see it in his eyes. As Torre used to say, "It's a look that you don't teach."

Any conversation about the greatness of Jeter includes the famous flip play. It came in Game 3 of the 2001 American League Divison Series against the Oakland A's. This series had plenty of backstories coming into it. For starters it was rematch of the 2000 ALDS that the Yanks won in five games. Oakland's GM, Billy Beane—the famous subject of *Moneyball*—was back looking for revenge, sporting a team with a payroll ($34 million) that was less than one third of the Yankees ($112 million). For the Yankees there was the added weight and responsibility the players felt playing for their devastated city, which was still dealing with the horrendous aftermath of the attacks on September 11th.

With two outs in the bottom of the seventh inning, the Yankees nursed a 1–0 lead, their first lead of the series. They had already dug themselves a major hole, dropping the first two games in New York. No team in baseball history has ever come back in a best of five after losing the first two at home. Terrence Long cracked a Mike Mussina pitch down the first-base line. A's slugger Jeremy Giambi, who was on first, was off at the crack of the bat. The ball went into the right-field corner and bounced around before Shane Spencer tracked it down and came up firing. Both Soriano and Martinez were lined up as cutoff men. Spencer air-mailed it over both of them. The ball was going to land helplessly off line between first and home, a place where no one is traditionally stationed. And with Giambi chugging around third, Mussina was thinking the game would be tied.

But even though Jeter was positioned as a cutoff man for a play at third, he saw that Spencer's throw was going to land in no man's land and rushed over to do something about it. On a full sprint, he grabbed the ball on one hop. But he still had the problem of his momentum. Even with the ball in hand, his body was moving away from the play. Jorge Posada was waiting at home *behind* Jeter. Somehow Derek computed all of this in a fraction of a second. He made a backhand toss toward Posada that factored in his momentum, and the ball reached the front side of Posada, who grabbed it, swung his arm to the left, and tagged Giambi on the leg an instant before his foot came down on the plate.

Even watching it on replay now all these years later, you can't believe Jeter makes that play. And you can really hear the crowd at Oakland County Stadium basically go into shock. It was baseball's version of the Immaculate Reception, the famous play in the '72 NFL playoffs when the Steelers' Franco Harris caught a deflected Terry Bradshaw pass on his shoe tops and ran it in for the winning touchdown against the Raiders. Actually you could say Jeter's play was even better because not only did he have to track down and catch the errant ball, he also had to make a perfect throw.

For the Yankees it was a huge shot in the arm. What perhaps made it even a little bit sweeter was the man who had waved Giambi home was Oakland's third base coach, Ron Washington, the same man who said Jeter was "not no shortstop." Even before that play, Washington didn't need any convincing about his incorrect assessment years before. He'd come around to admit his mistake. But it was poetic justice nonetheless. It was a stunning play that turned the series around. Beane said, "Derek Jeter even has an elegant way of breaking your heart."

Derek wasn't done making signature plays in this series. In the top of the eighth inning in Game 5 and with the Yankees trying to hold on to a 5–3 lead, Oakland had a man on first and Long at the plate again. He skied one foul along third base. Both Scott Brosius and Jeter gave chase. The ball was going to land in the camera pit, but that didn't stop Derek. He leaned over to glove the ball, but the low wall hit him below the waist and he fell—head over cleats—into the pit before landing on his back on the cement floor. You could hear the anxiety in the Yankees crowd. *Did we just lose our captain?* Not a chance. Derek made the catch, got the out. The Yankees would win the game and the series. Jeter's play not only inspired the team and the city, but also inspired another great line from Beane. "That's the heart of the Yankees aura," the GM said. "At no time did you think they're not going to come back and beat you."

I remember another time when Jeter's fearless pursuit of victory was on full display. It was July 1, 2004, and the Red Sox were in town. The two rivals were once again battling near the top of the standings. At the time the Red Sox shortstop was Nomar Garciapara. Nomar was forever being compared to Jeter. He'd won the AL Rookie of the Year in 1997, the year after Derek. He had put up better power numbers than Derek, but by this point, he was trailing in the World Series titles department 4–0. The Yankees won the first two games of the series and were looking for the sweep. So it was an important game for the Sox; however, Nomar opted not to play that night. He was given the chance, but he felt physically he couldn't make it. So he sat on the bench. Most of the rest of the team was on top step for most of the game. I remember thinking how lonely Nomar looked. It was clearly not a comfortable night for him. If I was in his shoes, I'd have been out there—unless I had a broken leg or something like that. Instead Garciapara sat and watched his nemesis steal the show.

The game went into extra innings. With two out in the top of the 12th inning and runners on second and third, pinch-hitter Trot Nixon popped up in foul territory along third base. Jeter once again took off on a sprint, coming all the way from second base. He made the catch in foul territory but couldn't slow down before running into the stands. He ended up diving face first into the crowd at practically full throttle. The speed at which he went in was unsettling because you knew that there was very little give in those box seats. Jeter ended up banging into some of those chairs riveted into the concrete with his face and shoulder. But once again he made the catch, ending the Red Sox rally. It also ended Derek's night. Jeter wanted to stay in the game, but looking more like he'd gone 12 rounds with Mike Tyson than 12 innings with Boston, he was taken straight to the hospital to treat cuts to his face and a bruised shoulder. After that inspiring dive and with their captain now on his way to the hospital, the Yankees rallied in the bottom of the 13th inning, scoring two to win the game 5–4. It was another standout moment among Jeter's many highlights during his career.

Derek gets a lot of credit for his achievements and deservedly so. But one area you don't hear much about is how he dealt with umpires. As far as I know, Derek was never thrown out of a game—ever. That's going all the way back to little league in Kalamazoo. Umpire John Hirschbeck knew a thing or two about ballplayers behaving badly. Roberto Alomar had spit in Hirschbeck's face in 1996. Of Jeter, Hirschbeck said: "In my 27 years in the big leagues, he is probably the classiest person I've ever been around." When you think of what a tough job the umps have, especially in this day and age of instant replay and social media second-guessing, at least they know there is one player on the field who won't show them up.

Derek could also make an announcer look good. I know I was lucky, but I'm still proud of the fact that back in the mid-to-late '90s I said, "I think Derek Jeter will be the Michael Jordan of baseball." In 2014, Jeter's final season, Nike began running a televised commercial called "RE2PECT" where famous New Yorkers thank Jeter for his tremendous career with a simple tip of their cap. There are politicians like Rudy Guliani and entertainers like Spike Lee, Billy Crystal, and Jay Z, all tipping their hats to Derek. Other athletes like Carmelo Anthony and Tiger Woods tip their hats. Even a Red Sox player at the time, Jon Lester, and some Boston fans—who have to stop rooting against the Yankees long enough to acknowledge Derek was a heck of player—tip their hats. Firemen, policemen, fans do the same. And the last man to tip his hat is...Michael Jordan. Sure, it's an ad, and all of those athletes are Nike guys. It doesn't change the fact that I said it almost 20 years ago. Now if I could only use that to land a Nike contract for myself.

Jeter was also the last standing of the so-called "Core Four." Derek, Posada, and pitchers Andy Pettitte and Rivera have a unique connection in Yankee-dom. They all were signed by the Yankees, came up through the minors, and all debuted with the big club in '95. They would end up all staying together as the core of the modern pinstripe dynasty team. It wasn't until 2004 when Pettitte left for a couple of seasons with the Astros that the core broke up briefly. Jeter, Posada, and Rivera stayed together for 17 years, the longest stretch of teammates playing together on the same team in the history of North American sports. Pettitte was back in pinstripes in 2007, and all four were on the roster for the 2009 championship. By the time Andy retired the first time after the 2010 season, the quartet had collected five World Series rings, seven AL pennants, and 11 AL East titles. Posada would hang 'em up the next year. Pettitte would come back for two more seasons and then retire along with Rivera in 2013. Derek was the last to go, completing his remarkable career in 2014, the end of a remarkable era of Yankees baseball.

On September 25, 2014—Jeter's final home game—the atmosphere at Yankee Stadium had a different feel. From the moment I arrived at 2:00 PM, five hours before game time, the concessionaires were unpacking T-shirts, towels, and jerseys saying "RE2PECT" in honor of Derek. The man, himself, arrived later than usual at probably 3:30. It was a weird scene with about 50 media members huddled near his locker, watching him change from his designer suit and tie into his uniform. I was kind of like, *Give the guy a little privacy*. He actually went into the training room to finish undressing and dressing. From a broadcast perspective, we made the unusual move of having a dedicated camera on Derek the entire evening from the time he arrived. Our boss Tony Pettiti's orders were: "Jeter, Jeter, Jeter…that's what this telecast is all about."

Producer Chris Pfeiffer told us there would be shorter commercial breaks and very few promo spots like a normal game. To me it was like a floating documentary. The close-up shots of the normally cool and composed Jeter, who was uncomfortable for the first time in his career, were fascinating. He took deep breaths, swallowed hard, and choked up. He went up the runway a few times between innings to release his emotions. My points to make before the game were to point out how he wore the uniform with no excessive bling, body art, nor crooked caps. He wore it in a way that made all of us who ever wore it before proud. I zeroed in on his signature fielding play, the one that Zimmer said he made better than any shortstop he had seen. But after an errant throw, it was already obvious he wasn't the graceful, fluid moving player he had been for 20 years.

Jeter, who always seemed so calm and in control of every situation even as a rookie, actually admitted that he had wished that manager Joe Girardi had taken him out in the ninth inning because he didn't want the ball hit to him. But instead divine intervention seemed to take place. The Baltimore Orioles tied it in the ninth inning, and he came through with his signature hit—a single to right field to win the game.

I was in the bullpen of the St. Louis Cardinals in 1982 and witnessed the last out of the World Series, which earned me a World Series ring. (And I waited longer than any player in any sport—even hockey star Ray Borque—to get that.) I was Pete Rose's pitching coach when Rose, a player/manager, broke Ty Cobb's all-time hit record. But Jeter's final home game was as emotional for me as any of those moments. After observing the final moments from the booth, I told Bob Costas that people paid large sums of money to witness this game, but I have watched Derek play over a thousand games in person and I got paid to do it. What a privilege.

When it's all said and done, Derek will be the all-time Yankees leader in hits, at-bats, stolen bases, and games played. He was selected to the All-Star Game 14 times and was named All-Star Game MVP—the first Yankee to receive that honor—in 2000. He was also World Series MVP that same year. Derek collected five Gold Gloves and five Silver Sluggers. He has more hits than any other shortstop in baseball history and more postseason hits than anyone to play the game. He was the Yankees captain for 12 of his 20 seasons. But he was also an inspiration to thousands upon thousands of kids. And a reminder to all of us that even in this age of PEDs, Twitter wars, holdouts, and supersized egos, it is still possible to play the game the right way and succeed.

When you look back at the most beloved Yankees of all time, other than the Babe, they are all products of the Yankees organization. Some of these homegrown talents like DiMaggio and Mantle were seen as stars from the start. Some, like Berra, needed a little big league seasoning before they could claim that status. Others, like Mattingly and Jeter, were almost traded away before they reached the majors. It makes you wonder if the next Yankees legend is about to come over the horizon a fully formed superstar? Or maybe he's already in the minor leagues, playing under the radar, wondering to himself how his number will look hanging in Monument Park. Just know it won't be a single digit, kid. I'm pretty sure all of those will be retired pretty darn soon.

CHAPTER 4
THE OUTFIELD

In the last few chapters we covered all the bases—literally. But when you look at a baseball field as a whole, you find something unique in all of sports. When you look at the other three major sports in the U.S., the field of play never changes. NFL football fields are 360 feet long (including end zones) by 160 feet wide. NBA basketball courts are all 94 by 50 feet. NHL rinks are now all 200 by 85 feet carbon copies of one another. What about baseball? Well, it's true that when it comes to the infields of all 30 major league stadiums, you are not going to find much in the way of physical variances. From the Rogers Centre in Toronto to Petco Park in San Diego and Seattle's Safeco Field to Marlins Park in Miami, your tape measure will tell you exactly the same thing. The bases are all 15 inches square and 90 feet apart. Every mound is 60 feet, six inches away and 10 inches above home plate.

But when you move to the outfield, everything changes. Here is where baseball expresses its personality. Among the thousands of rules and regulations in the official rules of baseball, there isn't one that explicitly defines the size, shape, distance from home, or the physical makeup of an outfield wall. (There, however, is a minimum distance of 250 feet, and MLB recommends 320 feet to foul poles and 400 feet to center field, but they are just suggestions.) That's why at Fenway you can have a 37-foot-tall Green Monster just 310 feet out in left field and a three-and-a-half-foot-wall around 380 feet out in right. A well-hit ball can bounce off of a scoreboard, a chain-link fence, or ivy-covered brick, depending on where you are playing. Short porches, death valleys, even a hill with a flagpole on it in play, you name it, baseball has it in the outfield. So it seems only fitting that some of the great personalities in the game were also found there. In this chapter we take a look at some of the unique characters who roamed the green expanse in the Bronx during my playing days, starting in the 1960s with "the Mick."

The Swingin' '60s

Mickey Mantle was a one-of-a-kind ballplayer. Just ask all the guys who were supposed to fill his shoes. He played 18 seasons (1951–68), all of them in New York and all of them hurt. And yet he still he put up some of most remarkable numbers in the game. He was a three-time American League MVP, was elected to 20 All-Star Games, and won the the 1956 Triple Crown. He is still the only switch-hitter to do the latter. He played in a dozen World Series, winning seven of them, and still owns several records for the Fall Classic. Casey Stengel said of Mickey, "He's got more natural power from both sides than anybody I ever saw." And Casey saw a lot.

Hall of Fame Yankees catcher Bill Dickey was more impressed with Mantle's speed, saying, "I expect to see that boy just take off and fly any time." Going down the first-base line after a hit, Mickey was clocked at 3.1 seconds. Most people can't do that from a sprinter's start. There are old clips of Mickey beating out a ground ball to second base for an infield single, and I'm not talking slow rollers deep in the hole. I mean balls sharply hit to the second baseman. He was something else, and just about all of his major accomplishments came after a devastating injury.

It was in Game 2 of the 1951 World Series when three of the biggest names in the game all came together on one play. The Yankees were playing the New York Giants, who were fresh off of Bobby Thomson's heroic shot to defeat the Brooklyn Dodgers. This was Mickey's rookie year, and he was playing right field because Joe DiMaggio still ruled center. But because Joe had lost a step or two, Casey Stengel told Mick to try and get every ball he could get his hands on. So when the great Willie Mays hit a pop-up to right-center field, Mickey was on his horse and coming full steam to catch it. But DiMaggio got there and was settling under the ball. Mick had to pull up. Unfortunately, the spikes on one of his cleats got stuck in a drain or a sprinkler cover or something, and it tore his knee up so bad that when he went down people thought

Mickey Mantle leans against the dugout steps during the rookie season of his Hall of Fame career, which included three MVPs.

he'd been shot. Some modern-day doctors now speculate that Mickey tore one of his knee ligaments that day. And since they didn't have the technology to repair them back then, it means he probably played most of his career without any lateral stability in his right knee. And he still put up those unbelievable numbers.

Mickey was also known as a great practical joker. If you asked him, "Hey, what's that guy's name over there that's waving at us?" Mickey would look at you straight faced and say, "Oh, that's Jimmy." So you'd go up to Jimmy, and say, "Hey Jimmy, how's it going? Good to see you again." And Jimmy would say, "My name is Dave." I was privileged to get to know Mickey very well in addition to pitching to him. Mickey was often our designated Par 3 player at our alumni golf events. He would stay on one tee and hit a shot for every group and pose for a picture. People just loved Mickey Mantle. Mickey came from a family of miners where the men all died young. That was one of the reasons he lived fast and loose, thinking his time was short. He drank a lot because he thought he was going to die from a hereditary cancer called Hodgkin's disease before the alcohol would ever get him. Unfortunately, he didn't know that his dad and granddad got sick from working in the mines and that breathing in all that lead and zinc dust helped bring on the cancer. Mickey used to joke that if he knew he was going to live as long as he did, he would've taken care of himself better, but there was some truth to that. The drinking eventually took its toll on his liver, and he was in really bad shape. I still have the memory of his plea to Yankees fans with a message on the Jumbotron after his liver transplant and just prior to his death. In the videotaped message, he said, "Look at me...I'm a role model of what you don't want to be." Seeing him look like that and then reflecting on what a powerful figure he was in the 1960s was quite a shock.

Mickey Charles Mantle died on August 13, 1995. The Yankees played the Cleveland Indians that night. Longtime Yankees organist Eddie Layton remembered Mickey telling him years ago that his favorite song was "Somewhere Over the Rainbow" from *The Wizard of Oz*. So that's what Eddie played that day. I bet it was hard to find a dry eye in the city that night.

The other iconic player in the Yankees outfield in the 1960s was Roger Maris. Most remember Roger for the 61 home runs he hit in 1961 and his season-long duel with Mickey, trying to catch Babe Ruth. Many forget that Roger was also a two-time AL MVP, a four-time All-Star, and a Gold Glove winner. Maris could do it all. But it was the No. 61 that will always be associated with this quiet man from North Dakota.

There were several big changes to the game that season. First off, the American League added two new teams, the Los Angeles Angels and a new Washington Senators team. (The team that I was on moved west to become the Minnesota Twins that season.) That meant there were more positions open in the majors. Suddenly pitchers who would've been in the minors were now throwing in the big leagues. They also added eight more games to the regular season of the American League that year to balance out the schedule. (The National League would do the same the following year when they added the Houston Colt .45's and the New York Mets.) Some see this perfect storm of changes to baseball as the sole reason Maris was able to pass Ruth for the most home runs in a single season. I don't think so. Sure, it helped, but every other hitter in the American League had those same conditions and none of them—including the Mick—could pass the Babe that year. And if you think about it, when Ruth hit his 60 home runs in 1927, he did it with the Murderer's Row lineup, a team with six Hall of Famers on it, as well as one on the bench, manager Miller Huggins.

Roger played seven seasons in the Bronx before being traded to St. Louis. He helped the Cardinals win the 1967 World Series, the third title of Roger's career. He retired from baseball the next year. I knew Roger very well. He used to visit the Cardinals' spring training camp in the early '80s when I was there because of his friendship with manager

Whitey Herzog. Nowadays, players participate in each others' charity events even if they are on opposing teams. That wasn't so much the case back then, but Roger—and Mickey, too—would be guys who would go out of their way to help every player they could. In 1983 Roger was diagnosed with, of all things, Hodgkin's disease—the same type of cancer that ran in Mantle's family. Roger died of that in 1985. He was only 51. But you can still see Mr. Maris when you go to Yankee Stadium. His retired No. 9 hangs out there in the outfield not far from his plaque in Monument Park.

Another memorable Yankee from the first half of my playing days was Bobby Murcer. Bobby played with the Yankees for parts of the '60s, '70s, and '80s. He was seen as the heir apparent to Mantle, having also come out of Oklahoma. He was even signed by the same scout, Tom Greenwade. His first major league hit in '65 was a home run to win the game. That was a good start, but he had some pretty big cleats to fill. Mickey retired in 1968 while Bobby was off fulfilling his military service. Murcer came back in 1969 and became the bridge between the Mantle and Mattingly eras. In fact he's the only Yankee to play with both. He was good with both the bat and glove. He led the league in putouts by an outfielder. He was a five-time All-Star and a Gold Glove winner. In 1970 Murcer became just the fourth Yankee to hit home runs in four consecutive at-bats, joining the likes of Gehrig, Johnny Blanchard, and Mantle.

In 1973 the Yankees gave Bobby, at the age of 26, a $100,000 contract. Up until then, only DiMaggio and Mantle had made six figures playing in pinstripes. But Bobby struggled during the two years the team played at Shea Stadium while Yankee Stadium was being refurbished. He was eventually traded to San Francisco after the 1974 season for Bobby Bonds. Murcer spent the next few years in the National League with the Giants and then the Chicago Cubs. On September 26, 1977, he hit the 200th career home run of his career off a tall left-handed pitcher for the Philadelphia Phillies—otherwise known as me. That's right. My future broadcast partner tagged me for his milestone home run. He was traded back to the Yankees in June of 1979, about a month after I arrived in the Bronx. I was there to witness both the best and worst moments of his career.

Bobby was very close friends with Thurman Munson. So when Thurman died in a plane crash that summer, it hit Bobby really hard. On August 6, 1979, George Steinbrenner, Billy Martin, and the entire team went to Thurman's funeral in Ohio. Bobby and Lou Piniella gave eulogies. It was a very emotional service, but afterward we all had to jump on a plane and fly back to New York for a game against the Baltimore Orioles that night. When we arrived, Billy Martin could see the toll the day had taken on Bobby and he asked if Bobby wanted to sit out the game. As drained as he was, Bobby told Billy that he wanted to play that night and that he'd dedicate the game to Thurman. The Yankees would rally to win that game 5–4, and all five runs came from the bat of Murcer. He hit a three-run homer in the seventh and followed that up with a two-run single in the bottom of the ninth to win the game. It was as gutsy a performance as I have ever seen.

A longtime fan favorite, Bobby retired in 1983 to make room for Don Mattingly at first. He would move right up into the booth, and Yankees fans got to enjoy years of his insightful commentary and unflinching honesty. Many remember that Bobby called the famous Pine Tar Game in July of '83. I learned a lot from him when I started my broadcasting career and I was honored to call part of my last game as a Yankees broadcaster with him in the booth in 2006. Unfortunately, a few months later Bobby was diagnosed with brain cancer. He battled, like the fighter he always was, and was back in the booth for Opening Day in 2007. But by the following summer, the cancer had returned, and Bobby died on July 12, 2008, just before the All-Star Game at Yankee Stadium. George Steinbrenner wasn't always known for his choice of words, but this time he got it right when he said, "Bobby Murcer was a born Yankee."

The Sensational '70s

When you think of the New York Yankees of the 1970s, the first name that comes to mind has to be Reggie Jackson. He famously said he was the "straw that stirs the drink" for the Yankees. Talented, smart, controversial, combustible, and, most of all, a clutch performer, he stirred up plenty of emotions in the locker room, the dugout, the front office, and all across New York. I don't know too many athletes who could have endured the blinding glare of the spotlight—the amount of good and bad press that Reggie got during his time in the Bronx—and still perform. When the chips were down, Reggie was the guy. Before the chips were down, well...that's another story.

Reggie was an interesting character from the start. He went to Arizona State University on a football scholarship but switched to baseball while there. The story goes that he tried out for the ASU baseball coach and hit several home runs while still wearing his football pads. Reggie was always a man of his convictions. He grew up in a predominantly Jewish neighborhood north of Philadelphia. And even though his family wasn't Jewish, he developed a strong bond with the community. It was so strong that after the massacre of Israeli athletes at the Munich Olympics in 1972, Reggie joined Jewish teammates Ken Holtzman and Mike Epstein on the Oakland A's in wearing black armbands during games. Reggie came to New York in 1977, having already won an American League MVP award in '73 as well as three World Series rings with the A's. "I didn't come to New York to be a star," Reggie said. "I brought my star with me." Saying things like that, you could see why Reggie rubbed some of his teammates the wrong way. When I was there, Catfish Hunter and Graig Nettles would needle Reggie with one-liners all the time. Even the old timers would get in on it. When Elston Howard was asked how Reggie would have fared on the great Yankees ballclubs of the '50s and '60s, Ellie's response was as measured as the man himself. "Fifth outfielder," he replied.

Reggie had several run-ins with manager Billy Martin—the most famous being when they almost came to blows in the dugout at Fenway Park in the summer of '77. Late in a blowout loss to the Boston Red Sox, Billy made a double switch of the pitcher and right fielder. You see this maneuver a lot in the National League because it allows you to move the pitcher's spot in the batting order. But since pitchers didn't bat in the American League, it was out of the ordinary. Billy was pulling Reggie because he thought he was loafing on a play. And one thing you never did on Billy's teams was give less than 100 percent. Billy only made it to the majors as a player because he worked so hard, so he expected the same work ethic from his players. Unlike Billy, Reggie was a natural at just about every sport he tried, so he had a different work ethic. When he was in Oakland, he showed off a good glove and a solid arm in the outfield. Those didn't seem as important to him in New York. So when he saw Paul Blair trotting out to replace him, he was not happy. Reggie came off the field, into the dugout, and went straight for Martin. Coaches Yogi Berra and Howard pulled them apart, and someone threw a towel over the camera in the dugout to try and keep it from the national TV audience, but other cameras caught it. No punches were thrown, but that was life in the Bronx Zoo.

Reggie also had a running feud with catcher and Yankees captain Thurman Munson. So it's ironic that Thurman was the one who gave Reggie his famous nickname. In 1977 reporters were pestering Munson as the team made their second straight postseason appearance. Of course, Reggie had even more experience from his days in Oakland. So Thurman wondered aloud to reporters if Reggie might not be a better person to answer questions on the subject. He told some members of the press to "Go ask Mr. October." It was said sarcastically, but a few days later, Reggie turned it into a perfect nickname with an incredible performance. Most people know about Reggie's three home runs in Game 6 that solidified the nickname. What many forget is that Reggie did that against three different pitchers and with just three swings of the bat. And what even fewer people recall is Reggie walked his first time in that game on four pitches, and he hit a home run his last at-bat in Game 5. So on four consecutive swings, he hit a home run in the World Series. Love him or hate him, you have to tip your hat to a man who can do that.

Jackson also had a pretty stormy relationship with George Steinbrenner that continued throughout his time in New York. They won the pennant again in the strike-shortened '81 season. Reggie hurt himself in the American League Championship Series while defeating the A's, then managed by Martin. Reggie would miss the first two games of the World Series against the Los Angeles Dodgers, and the Yankees won both games. Steinbrenner then supposedly had Reggie benched for Game 3 even after he was medically cleared to play. That's an odd choice, considering his nickname and the time of year. The Dodgers would win that game and the next three to take the title. Reggie left for the California Angels after that. By the time he retired with the A's in 1987, Reggie had played 21 seasons, winning six pennants and five championships. He had 563 home runs and 2,584 hits in his career. Of course he also collected 2,597 strikeouts; that's 13 more whiffs than hits. A 14-time All-Star, he was elected to Cooperstown in 1993. And you'll never see a No. 44 in pinstripes again as it was retired by the Yankees that same year.

In the years since, Reggie has stayed involved with the organization. He's a frequent face at Old Timers' Day. In 2008, before Reggie threw out the ceremonial first pitch to start the final season at the old Yankee Stadium, he made a strange request. He asked that Yogi come out to the mound with him. Reggie's track record with the Yankees had plenty of ups and downs. Many in the dugout thought this was Reggie's way of ensuring he wasn't booed because no one ever boos Yogi. More recently, Jackson has worked for the Yankees as a special assistant and is often seen at spring training. He was one of several former Yankees who talked to A-Rod and Jeter when they were having difficulties. Reggie also got in some hot water when he said in a *Sports Illustrated* article in 2012 that, as much as he likes A-Rod, there is some doubt about the numbers he put up. Even in retirement Reggie still finds a way to "stir the drink" every now and again.

When I played with the Yankees, Reggie was a fixture in right field. And to his right was the other Mickey to hold down center field in the Bronx. Mickey Rivers, aka "Mick the Quick," was one of the fastest men to put on pinstripes. Rivers was traded to the Yankees along with Ed Figueroa after the 1975 season for Barry Bonds' father, Bobby. Rivers covered center for the Yankees during their back-to-back titles. He was traded to the Texas Rangers soon after I got to the Bronx, but it didn't take long to appreciate the speed he had out there or his wicked sense of humor. Near the end of Catfish Hunter's career when he was basically pitching on fumes—though still pitching and never begging out—Mickey Rivers would take the field and assume a sprinter's stance with his back to the infield, basically insinuating that the ball would be hit over his head because Cat had been getting hit pretty hard of late. It was all done in good fun, but that was Mickey. Another time when Reggie told a reporter that he had an IQ of 160, Mickey's reply was, "Out of what, 1,000?" Clearly his tongue was as quick as his feet.

Oscar Gamble was another guy quick with a joke and one of the funniest guys you could be around. The "Big O," as Phil Rizzuto called him, had two stints with the Yankees—1976 and again from 1979–1984. He also loved to needle Reggie. Jackson hit behind Oscar in the batting order and he would often draw a walk. When Oscar got back to the dugout, he'd tell Reggie that they pitched around him to get to Reggie. Oscar called himself the "ratio man." Because he was often platooned, he would come to bat only 200 times a season but hit 20 home runs, or one about every 10 at-bats, the best ratio in the league. Many remember Oscar for his crazy, hunched-over batting style and the large Afro upon which he wore his Yankee hat, but the man could really swing a mean bat as well.

There were a couple of other notable guys who worked the outfield in the '70s. Roy White spent his entire MLB career as a Yankee. During his 15 seasons from 1965–1979, he was voted to two All-Star teams and won two World Series titles in the '70s. Roy was the kind of guy that every winning team needs to have: a switch-hitter who could play any position in the outfield. Roy had a great eye at the plate and always did the little things. He led the league in walks one year and sacrifice flies another. Paul Blair also donned the pinstripes in the '70s. He had won two World Series and eight Gold Gloves in Baltimore before being traded to the Yankees in 1977. I always wondered if Martin had not sent Paul out to replace Reggie that day in Fenway, if Billy and Reggie would have even gotten into a shouting match. Paul's nickname was "Motormouth." So if he was still on the bench, I'm not sure Reggie or Billy could have gotten a word out.

Lou Piniella was one of my favorite teammates when I played in New York. His banter with Graig Nettles on the team bus rides was priceless. He played the last 11 of his 18 big league seasons with the Yankees as an outfielder and designated hitter. He was an anchor for those "Bronx Zoo" years. "Sweet Lou" was the AL Rookie of the year in 1969 with the up-start Kansas City Royals. In fact, Lou got the very first hit in Royals history. He made the All-Star team in '72 as well. Lou always had a head for the game. Only two years after retiring from playing for the Yankees, he was back managing the team in 1986 and '87. The next year he was bumped up to general manager before ending up back in the dugout, replacing Billy Martin after one of his numerous firings. Lou ended up winning another World Series as manager of the Cincinnati Reds in 1990 to go with the two he won as a player in New York. One of Lou's best performances on the bench was as skipper for the 2001 Seattle Mariners. His team tied an MLB record for wins with 116 that season. But he would be upset in the ALCS that year by Derek Jeter and the Yankees in five games.

Empty in the '80s

The next decade could be considered the Dark Ages in Yankees history. It was the first decade since the team played at the Polo Grounds that they failed to win at least one World Series. Their only glimmer of greatness was the 1981 pennant they won, so at least that streak of capturing pennants every decade still stretches back to the 1920s. Despite the lean years (at least by Yankees standards), they had some great athletes on the roster. In fact, they might have had the single best athlete in Yankees history on the team for most of the '80s. And his name was Dave Winfield. How good was Winfield? Well, coming out of college he was drafted by four different leagues in three different sports. In 1973 the San Diego Padres selected Dave—as a pitcher—with the fourth pick of the Major League Baseball draft. Dave had also been a part of a Big Ten champion basketball team when he was at the University of Minnesota, so it was little surprise that the Atlanta Hawks of the NBA and the Utah Stars of the old ABA each took a chance and drafted him. The big surprise was the NFL. Dave never played a single down of football in college, and yet the Minnesota Vikings used a late-round pick on him in the draft that year. Of course, at 6'6" and 220 pounds, I'm sure he would've done pretty well, no matter where he ended up. To this day, he remains the only athlete to be drafted by four different leagues. Baseball should feel lucky they got him.

The Padres quickly moved Dave to right field so they could get his bat in the lineup every game and where they could still use his cannon for an arm throwing out people from the outfield. After eight seasons in San Diego, where he was a four-time All-Star and two-time Gold Glove winner, Winfield became a free agent. And we all know how George Steinbrenner likes talented free agents. In December of 1980, George signed Dave to a 10-year, $23 million deal, the richest contract in the game at the time. He was earning more than twice as much as the next highest guy on the team, pitcher Tommy John. The Yankees reached the World Series in Winfield's first season, and Dave had a solid postseason both in the field and at the plate—something a lot of detractors would forget in the coming years. The Yankees lost that series to the Dodgers. It wasn't long before many of the important pieces of the '70s dynasty teams—Reggie Jackson, Bucky Dent, Graig Nettles, and Goose Gossage—were gone.

During his first five seasons in New York, he was the best run producer in the league. In 1984 he and teammate Don Mattingly battled for the league batting title all the way to the final game of the season. Mattingly won it by three points by going 4-for-5 that day. Dave also stirred up a bit of controversy in 1983 when he killed a seagull after hitting it with a thrown baseball in Toronto. Dave maintained it was an accident, but he was charged with cruelty to animals by Canadian authorities. When asked about the incident, Billy Martin famously quipped, "It's the first time he's hit the cutoff man all season." Charges were later dropped, but during the offseason, Winfield went back up to Toronto to raise more than $60,000 for Easter Seals. Still, any time he played at Exhibition Stadium, the Blue Jays fans let him have it with insults and arm-flapping taunts for years afterward. That was until Dave became a member of the Blue Jays and helped lead them to their first World Series title in 1992. Suddenly, all was forgiven by our neighbors to the north, and Dave became a fan favorite.

My first stint as a Yankees announcer came as Winfield was starting the second half of his 10-year contract. In 1986 I was calling games on WPIX with Phil Rizzuto and Bill White. On Opening Day we were hosting the Kansas City Royals. The Yanks were leading 4–2 in the bottom of the eighth inning when he stepped to the plate. Willie Randolph and Don Mattingly had hit back-to-back singles and were standing on first and second. Facing Kansas City's side-armed closer Dan Quisenberry and with a chance to blow the game wide open, Winfield tried to bunt. So I said on the air, "Wow, that's a surprise. A big guy like that—a major run producer—and he is trying to drop down a bunt?" Winfield ended up hitting into a double play, but the Yankees held on to win the game 4–2.

The next day, an article by Dick Young—a famous sportswriter in New York at the time—hit the newsstands. Dick never avoided controversy if he could help it, and if there wasn't a controversy, by gosh, he would create one. So he writes about a rookie broadcaster who was not afraid to criticize Winfield and say what a bad play trying to bunt was. I, of course, was the rookie broadcaster in his story. So people were saying to me, "Did you see Dick Young's story? What are you going to do about it?" Well, I had always been told by one of my broadcast mentors, the legendary Tim McCarver, that if you say anything controversial or something that upsets a player, make sure you are in locker room the next day in case they have something they want to say about it. Make yourself available to them. So that's what I did. I went down to the clubhouse, wondering what the reaction was going to be. There I saw Dave, flashing that famous big grin of his. "I heard what you said, Jim. There wasn't anything critical about that." That defused the situation right then and there. Young wouldn't get his controversy this time. But it was great early training for me about how things can get distorted by what people think you said over the air versus what you actually did say. As an announcer you could say 20 very complimentary things about a player, but if you do happen to say one critical thing, that could upset him and probably cause a confrontation.

Although I didn't upset Winfield that time, I apparently wasn't "Yankee enough" (whatever that means) for Steinbrenner, and my contract as a broadcaster of Yankees games was not renewed. Billy Martin took my place in the Yankees booth, and I went off to work with the Minnesota Twins for the next six seasons and ended up covering Winfield again when joined the Twins in 1993. Dave had his own issues with Steinbrenner. There was the infamous "Mr. May" comments that George made, negatively comparing Winfield's traditional strong starts to the season with Reggie's "Mr. October" postseason heroics. Those comments never sat well. And the two disagreed for years about a payment to Winfield's charity that George was contractually obligated to make. Things got so bad that George hired Howard Spira—a known gambler with ties to the Mafia—to dig up dirt to discredit Winfield. When the league found out about that, George was banned from the team in July of 1990. But by then Winfield had left for the Angels.

Dave ended up playing for six different teams during his 22 seasons in the big leagues. When I was a player, I was traded and sold five times during my 25-year career, so I knew what that was like. But Winfield can claim one unique distinction on me—and any other major league ballplayer for that matter. In 1994 Dave was traded from the Twins to the Indians for a player to be named later, while the players were out on strike. That season was eventually canceled, World Series and all, so Dave never played for Cleveland, and no player was ever sent to Minnesota. Finding themselves in an unusual situation of an incomplete trade due to the strike, the teams were rumored to have decided to settle things in a unique way. The executives of the Indians took the Twins' top brass out to a meal and picked up the check. So Winfield may be the only player who was ever traded for a dinner. Despite all the bad blood with Steinbrenner, Winfield let it all go. Dave did enter the Hall of Fame as a Padre in 2001. In 2008 he participated in both the final Old Timers' Day ceremony and the final game ceremony at the Old Yankee Stadium.

Rickey Henderson is another Hall of Famer who prowled the outfield grass at Yankee Stadium during the 1980s. It's said that Rickey was born in the back of a car on the way to the hospital, so I guess he was moving pretty fast from the start. He played for the Bombers from 1985–1989 sandwiched between stints in Oakland. He came over from the A's with pitcher Bert Bradley for five players: utility man Stan Javier, and pitchers Tim Birtsas, Jay Howell, Jose Rijo, and Eric Plunk. When New York traded him back to Oakland in June of '89, it received outfielder Luis Polonia and pitcher Greg Cadaret, as well as getting Plunk back. Rickey had a special talent when it came to stealing bases. Rickey ran away with the Yankees team record, collecting 326 in a little over four seasons in the Bronx. The old record was 248 set by Hal Chase, who played back in the early 1900s when the Yankees were still called the Highlanders. Derek Jeter now owns the franchise mark, but to pass Rickey he needed *2,100* more games. Rickey also had a penchant for referring to himself in the third person. He'd say things like, "If Rickey wants to steal a base, Rickey's gonna steal that base." And Rickey stole a lot of bases. When he finally stopped playing in 2003, at the age of 44 after 25 seasons with nine different teams—including three stints with the A's and two with the Padres—Rickey had collected a major league record 1,406 stolen bases, including the single-season mark of 130. He was elected to Cooperstown on the first ballot in 2009.

The New Look '90s

The 1980s were a decade where the Yankees often traded away their young prospects in order to land more established talents. It was a practice that netted them exactly zero World Series titles. And Steinbrenner rarely wanted to wait for players to develop. But after the Winfield/Spira fiasco, George was banned from everyday operations of the team at the start of the decade. Suddenly, the Yankees could keep the talent they were developing and bring them along in the time-honored fashion of baseball. George's lifetime ban would be lifted after only two years, but by then Gene Michael, Bob Watson, Brian Cashman, and several other baseball men in the organization had built the infrastructure that could withstand even George's meddling. It came to be known as the "Core Four" era thanks to Derek Jeter, Jorge Posada, Andy Pettitte, and Mariano Rivera...But you should really include the guy who came up first and started it all. And he did it in center field.

Bernie Williams is one of the sweetest people you would ever want to know. Soft-spoken and humble, his quiet demeanor was so un-New York-like that Bernie was almost traded several times in his career. But the Yankees kept him, and he ended up authoring some great Yankees moments in the '90s. Like his two home runs—one from each side of the plate against the Texas Rangers—to win the Yankees' first playoff series in 17 seasons. His 11th inning home run against the Baltimore Orioles eventually won Game 1 of the '96 ALCS, following the nortorious Jeffrey Maier incident when a fan reached over the fence. Williams was named MVP of that series.

Bernie was born and raised in Puerto Rico and was signed by the Yankees in 1985 on his 17th birthday. He broke in with the big club in '91 and was the starting center fielder by '93. From 1996–2001 Bernie won four World Series rings, made five All-Star teams, earned four Gold Gloves, and won an AL batting title. In fact, in '98 Bernie became the first player ever to collect a batting title, a Gold Glove, and a World Series title in the same season. A very cerebral man, he considered studying to become a doctor while he played minor league ball. Occasionally, he would drift into a zone that his teammates lovingly called "Bernie's World." But even though they understood it, they didn't always like it. Bernie was off in his own world before Game 6 of the 2001 World Series and showed up late to pregame warm-ups in Arizona. Jeter gave him an earful that day. Becasue he was so mad, he didn't follow his usual protocol and do it behind closed doors. It was one of the few times that Derek's rebuke of a player was caught by the media.

Bernie was one of the nicest guys on the planet, so I was surprised one day walking through the clubhouse when Bernie stopped me and said, "I want to ask you something. Why do you say I cheat?"

My first reaction was, "What are you talking about? I never said that, Bernie."

"Yes. You say I peek at the pitches."

For those who don't know, "peeking" at pitches is a no-no in baseball. It means that when the catcher is sending signs to the pitcher for what pitch to throw next, the batter glances back there to see the sign or

Though he could be a bit spacey, outfielder Bernie Williams won four World Series rings, made five All-Star teams, earned four Gold Gloves, and won an AL batting title during a six-year period.

where the catcher is setting up. If the batter knows what pitch is coming or whether it's headed for the inside corner or the outside corner, he obviously has an advantage he is not supposed to have. There is no official rule against it. It's more of one of those unwritten rules.

We had a way of dealing with that when I was pitching. If we thought the batter was trying to see our signs, we would have the catcher sit way outside and up close to the plate. The batter would see the catcher out of the corner of his eye and think the pitch was coming low and away. We had a pre-arranged signal with the catcher to throw it up and in. So when the hitter leaned in for a pitch he thought was low and outside, it came at him—usually not too far from his chin. That usually discouraged him from trying to steal signs. The great Dodgers and Padres first baseman Steve Garvey was known for peeking. Bernie also had that rep. So I explained to Bernie, "I didn't say you cheat. I just reported what I heard from several managers. You have a reputation around the league. Whether you mean to do it or not, I don't know. But they say you will—with good timing—look back at the catcher while he's giving the sign. And then if you get a hit, the opposing manager is going to think you are peeking." Bernie, of course, got a lot of timely hits so there was a lot for managers to be grousing about.

Like Jeter, Posada, and Rivera of the Core Four, Bernie played his entire 16-year career in the Bronx. I'm very happy Bernie had a great career because I had heard he was taunted unmercifully by Yankees teammate Mel Hall when he came up from the minors. Don Mattingly was very supportive of him during this time, which is not surprising. But even then the bullying got so bad that the Yankees let Hall go at the end of '92 season. (He ended up playing in Japan.) Soon after, Bernie's career began to take off. It's even more impressive when you reflect on what Bernie has accomplished as a switch-hitting center fielder in the Bronx after Yankees fans had been disappointed by many of the so-called "next Mickey Mantles." Bill Robinson, Roger Repoz, and Ross Moschitto all were ticketed for stardom but ended up as busts.

Bernie was a track star and an accomplished classical guitarist. He performed at the first Opening Day at the new Yankee Stadium, as well as playing the national anthem before a New Jersey Nets game in 2011. He has also been nominated for a Grammy. Bernie wasn't necessarily blessed with as many baseball skills as some of his peers, but with smart and long practice, he became a batting champion and an outstanding Yankees center fielder.

Paul O'Neill wasn't an original Yankee, but he sure left his mark in the Bronx. He's been a good friend since our days in Cincinnati together. I was Pete Rose's pitching coach for part of 1984–85. I was there to see Paul get his first big league hit as a rookie with Reds. I said to Pete Rose, "That kid has the sweetest swing I've seen since Ted Williams." He was also a really heads-up player. Paul would win a World Series with the Reds in 1990 before being traded to New York in November of 1992 for Roberto Kelly, one of the Yankees' best trades, in my opinion. Paul was a perfectionist when it came to his hitting. His .359 average in '94 led the league. Every trip to the plate was important for him. Pitcher Jim Morris was made famous in the Disney movie *The Rookie* because he improbably made it to big leagues in his mid-30s after teaching and coaching high school for years. Well, Morris once struck out Paul. After which Paul went into the dugout and started bashing his helmet, saying, "I got struck out by a f----- school teacher!"

Yogi Berra used to say, "90 percent of the game is half-mental." Though he messed up the math, that notion is true for a lot of sports really. When I was broadcasting for the Yankees, my golf game started having some issues. So I went to see a sports hypnotist in New York named Pete Solana to help with the mental side of my golf game. Not long after that, O'Neill was coming off the 21-day disabled list. I was calling his first game back, so I said, "One of challenges for Paul is going to be kind of lowering expectations and not feeling like he's going to go 5-for-5." He is so intense, Joe Torre used to say, "Paul isn't happy unless he goes 6-for-5." He just hated to give up an at-bat. So in his first game back, what does Paul do? He hits four solid line drives and gets three hits. I hadn't seen him that relaxed at the plate in a long time. So much for my prognosticating. The next day I get call from Solana. He said, "Did Paul mention that I worked with him?"

I had no idea that Paul and Pete knew each other. So I asked Paul, "Do you know Pete Solana?"

"Oh yeah, sure. We play racquetball together. He got my mind right for coming back into the lineup." He sure did.

Many major league players can go their whole career without ever being a part of a no-hitter. And with only 23 perfect games thrown in all of baseball history, even fewer have ever gotten to witness that rare spectacle from the winning dugout. O'Neill has...*three times*. He was there when Tom Browning threw one for the Reds in '88 and registered the final putout for David Wells' bit of perfection 10 years later. And in '99 he made a beautiful diving catch in right field to help preserve David Cone's perfect game at Yankee Stadium. Some guys get all the luck.

Another big name roaming the outfield in the Bronx in the '90s first made a name for himself across town in Queens. Darryl Strawberry was the National League Rookie of the Year with the Mets in 1983 and won his first World Series with them, stunning Bill Buckner and the Red Sox in 1986. Straw came to the Yankees after a drug suspension in 1995 and he would miss some time with the club while being treated for colon cancer. But when they needed him, Darryl was there. And along with former teammates Cone and Doc Gooden, he seemed to find some of that old Mets magic in the Bronx in the late '90s, helping the Yankees on their remarkable run. Now an ordained Christian minister, Darryl speaks all around the country about the mistakes he made early in his career, hoping to inspire other young athletes to avoid making the same ones.

Some Yankees outfielders are memorable for all the wrong reasons. Chad Curtis is one of those. Chad made some good plays on the field and was one of many left fielders who contributed to the Yankees championships But Curtis was a strange dude. Though a religious man, he once called out Jeter for *not* fighting during a brawl with the Seattle Mariners in August of '99. After a few hit batsmen, Mariners pitcher Frankie Rodriguez charged Yankees catcher Joe Girardi, and the benches emptied. Curtis was right in the middle of the mayhem. As for Derek, he ended up squared off with A-Rod, who was with Seattle at the time. The two were good friends back then, so they didn't throw any punches at each other. Later, Curtis was incensed and yelled at Jeter for being too friendly to the opposition. Chad always had a different look in his eye.

Millennium Men

My first season in the majors was 1959, the year the Red Sox became the last team to integrate their roster and 12 long years after Jackie Robinson broke the color barrier. Throughout my career I saw the growth of Latino players in the bigs as teams tapped into the rich talent pools of Central and South American nations as well as the Caribbean. As an announcer I now have seen the majors focus their attention on Asia. It's very common for teams to have at least one player from Japan, Korea, or Taiwan on their rosters. A fourth of the players in the game today are foreign born, which I think is great for the game. The deeper the talent pool, the better the games. The foreign countries best represented are the Dominican Republic, Venezuela, and Cuba. And with all of those countries speaking Spanish, players usually have several buddies on their team that they can communicate with, so it's not as critical for them to learn English. For Asian players it is a different story. And it is one of the reasons I am so fond of Hideki Matsui.

Matsui was a superstar in Japan before coming to New York. He played 10 seasons there, winning three championships and numerous awards. His team, the Yomiuri Giants, offered him the richest contract in their league's history to stay with them. But Matsui wanted to test himself against the best in the world so he turned it down and took less money to become a Yankee. It was one of the few times that Steinbrenner paid less than the other guy and still got his man.

Matsui arrived in the Bronx in 2003. And while he always had his interpreter, Roger, with him, he worked hard at learning English so he could communicate with his teammates, coaches, and the media. I instantly gravitated toward him. For a person not used to the language and the customs here, his polite and accessible ways were much appreciated. He made a conscious effort to learn the names of the members of the media. He seemed to go about everything the right way. Hideki was probably the most respected of all the Japanese players who became Yankees. I'll never forget his first game at Yankee Stadium. It was the home opener in 2003 against the Minnesota Twins. Matsui came up with the bases loaded in the bottom of the fifth inning. I remember commenting on his "rock star persona" and how these are the moments at which he excels. He belted the next pitch from Joe Mays over the right-field wall. The booth literally shook from the reaction of Yankees fans. He became the first guy in pinstripes to hit a grand slam in his Yankee Stadium debut. New York...meet Godzilla.

As big a star as he was in Japan, Hideki really worked hard at his craft and came to play every day. Early in the '06 season, Matsui broke his wrist trying to make a sliding catch in the outfield. At the time of the injury, he had never missed a game in his professional career, going back to 1993 in Japan. That's 1,768 games in a row! The man was a warrior. And yet Matsui apologized to the team that he wouldn't be able to play for a while. Can you imagine Reggie Jackson doing that? Jeter for one couldn't believe it, and it only added to their strong friendship. Jeter called Matsui, "one of my favorite teammates I've ever played with."

Matsui spent seven seasons in New York and, like a true rock star, he saved his best performance for last. During the 2009 World Series, the Yankees were taking on the defending champion Philadelphia Phillies. Matsui was the designated hitter, so he only started in the three games at Yankee Stadium because the pitchers had to bat when they played in Philly. Still, he was able to set or tie a whole bunch of Yankees records. He hit .615 for the series. He drove in six runs in one game, becoming the first Yankees player to do that since Bobby Richardson in 1960. The Yankees won the Series in six games, and Matsui was named World Series MVP, the first Japanese player and first DH to receive the honor. And he became just the third player in major league history to hit over .500 and hit three home runs in a World Series. The other two were Babe Ruth and Lou Gehrig. Matsui would play another three years in the majors, signing one-year contracts with the Angels, A's, and Rays, and then he signed a one-day contract with New York because he wanted to retire as a Yankee. I am glad he did.

Another outfielder from the millennium with an interesting story is Melky Cabrera. This kid started the 2005 season with the Yankees' Double A affiliate, the Trenton Thunder. But he played his way up to the Columbus Clippers, the Yankees' Triple A affiliate in Ohio. After a couple of weeks there, he made it up to the big club on July 7. Unfortunately, his rocket ride to the top only mirrored his trip back down. He was sent back down to Columbus less than 10 days later and then back down again to Trenton. So Melky started and ended the season in Double A. Let's face it, folks; baseball is a tough game. Cabrera's big break came in the form of Matsui's broken wrist. Back with the Yankees in '06, the 21-year-old Dominican hit the first walk-off home run of his young career, becoming the youngest Yankee to hit one since a 21-year-old Mickey Mantle did it way back in '53. Melky would have a very up-and-down career in pinstripes. But his bat would keep him around. He would hit the first walk-off at the new Yankee Stadium, a two-run shot in the bottom of the 14th inning to beat the A's 9–7 in April of '09. Later that season he became the first Yankees player to hit for the cycle since Tony Fernandez did it back in '95.

Another 21st century player, Nick Swisher, was a throwback kind of player. I played against his dad, Steve, who caught for the Cubs, Cardinals, and Padres for nine seasons in the '70s and early '80s. Nick was raised on the old ways of the game. He knew the big advantage that Yankees players had in spring training—being able to have legends like Reggie Jackson, Goose Gossage, and Yogi Berra there to give advice. In 2010 Nick had been struggling at the plate, often getting killed by breaking balls. He was doing what players do these days, which is analyze his swing from every possible way with stats, photographs, computers, etc. One day Yogi pulled him aside and simply told him, "Move up in the batter's box." By stepping closer to a breaking ball pitcher, Nick was swinging on the ball before it broke. It worked. Nick started hitting again. His average ended up being 40 points higher than the year before, and Nick earned an All-Star nod. It also demonstrated Yogi's specialty: saying a lot with a little.

Jim Kaat's All-Time Yankees Roster Now that we've gone around the diamond, it's time for my all-time team. This team draws from the years I've been around baseball—1959–2014. Ruth, Gehrig, and DiMaggio aren't listed. I'm not *that* old. I'll give you my top three in order at each position. This is the Yankees team I would want on the field if we had to win the World Series and our lives depended on it—in order to save the planet from, say, an alien invasion.

Catcher I think any conversation on Yankees catchers has to begin and end with **Yogi Berra**. He was the whole package. He could, hit, throw, field, and was excellent at calling games and handling pitchers. He was an amazing study. Nothing got by Yogi, so he'd be help even by sitting on the bench. And getting an occasional Yogi-ism is just an added bonus.

As his backups, I'd have **Elston Howard**, an appropriate choice, considering he was Yogi's real-life understudy. He was also the 1963 MVP. And I'd have **Thurman Munson**. "Tugboat" was as tough as they come and a great teammate. His leadership would be a big plus. And you could count on Tug for a clutch hit.

First Base I'd have to go with **Don Mattingly**. Donnie Baseball, like Yogi, was the total package. He never got a lot of big-game experience as a player, but when he did finally get to the postseason, he hit over .400. So I have to figure that he'd come through against the aliens.

Backing him up I'd have **Tino Martinez**. He was very underrated as a fielder and a leader in the clubhouse and a class guy who would do anything for the team. And I'd have **Chris Chambliss**. It's not really a step down at all if you had to put the "Snatcher" in late in a game. And if anyone knows what one swing of a bat can do, it's Chris.

Second Base Once again, I find myself going old school by picking **Bobby Richardson** mostly because of his outstanding ability to turn the double play. They don't call it the "pitcher's best friend" for nothing.

I'd go with **Willie Randolph** as the primary backup because of his smarts and his durability. And then I'd go with **Robinson Cano**. I know you're saying, "Cano has way better numbers than the other two. He's a superstar." I'll agree. He is talented beyond the other two, but he's also not as durable. And for all the numbers he puts up, Robbie is not as good at doing the little things that win ballgames like Willie and Bobby.

Third Base   Third base is both really hard and a piece of cake. It's hard because very little separates my top three choices. But it's easy because no matter who you start you have a rock solid guy holding down the hot corner. If I have to pick, I'd go with **Scott Brosius**. I saw firsthand on a daily basis the unbelievable plays and clutch hits Scott got during his short time in New York.

Of course, you can't go wrong with my backups, **Graig Nettles** and **Clete Boyer**. "Puff"—as we called Graig—and Clete both had some home run power, and both were great on the backhand play. I might give Puff a slight edge because of his long ball ability.

Shortstop   There's not much more to say here other than **Derek Jeter**. I was in No. 2's corner from early on. He was a winner—plain and simple. That's why I said he was going to become to baseball what Michael Jordan was to basketball. (And since Jordan defeated aliens in *Space Jam*, we should absolutely have Derek on board.)

To back up Jeter, I'd go with **Tony Kubek** and **Bucky Dent**. Tony probably won't surprise many people, but Bucky might. I got to play with him on two teams. I'm not picking him just because of his famous home run over the Green Monster. I'm picking him because his was a very steady glove in the field. That's something you can't underestimate.

Left Field   This one is tough because the Yankees didn't really have an everyday, 150-games-a-year guy during my baseball lifetime. The man with the most tenure in left was probably **Roy White**. So I'll give him the nod for his speed and experience.

For his backup I'd go with **Hideki Matsui**. He was sensational for the short term. After Matsui I'm not sure who to pick. Maybe I'd go with **Lou Piniella**. In case I get fired by George Steinbrenner, it would be good to have another former Yankees manager on the bench.

Center Field As Bob Sheppard would say: "Now batting, number 7...**Mickey Mantle**." I'm taking "the Mick" even with his bad knees. If I can have him with good knees, I might not need anyone else to beat the aliens.

Behind him on the depth chart, I'd have **Bernie Williams**, the best to roam center since Mantle, and then the *other* Mickey— **"Mick the Quick" Rivers**. A little speed on the base paths is always a good thing.

Right Field I'd start **Roger Maris** but not because he hit 61 home runs. Roger was a complete player with or without the milestone. He could run the bases, hit the cutoff man, and chase down fly balls. He wasn't a two-time MVP by accident.

I'd have **Reggie Jackson** as the first backup. Reggie liked a big stage, and I'm not sure what could be bigger than playing for the survival of Earth. But his fielding ability and legs were not what they were in Oakland in his early years. **Paul O'Neill** would be third. Paulie brought an intensity to the field every day and was, like Roger, a complete player. He was just not as good a base runner as Roger. I'd give my honorable mention to **Dave Winfield**. Big Dave had multiple years of 30-plus home runs and 100 RBIs and a cannon for an arm.

Pitchers For my starting rotation, I'll start with the left-handed pitchers. **Whitey Ford** still has one of the lowest ERAs and the best winning percentage in baseball history. **Andy Pettitte** is my first backup lefty because he is a big-game guy—just as long as he's not tipping his pitches. **Ron Guidry** was the ultimate team player, who was as good as they come throwing the ball.

For right-handed pitchers, I'd select **"Catfish" Hunter**. He was one of the most unhittable pitchers in his prime. Then I'd pick **Mel Stottlemyre**. He is probably better known as a pitching coach, but he had three 20-win seasons during his 11 years with the Yankees. He was a very tough sinkerball pitcher. If his playing days weren't cut short by an arm injury, you wouldn't be thinking twice about my choice here. No. 3 is a tie between **David Cone** and **David Wells**. These two guys were gamers. I'd take them into battle any day.

My bullpen would have **Sparky Lyle** and **Goose Gossage** as set-up men. I know they were closers in their prime, but when you have **Mariano Rivera**—which I do—on your staff, you have to go with Mo as the closer. He's the best ever and a heck of a guy.

Not Making the Roster My most notable omission is **Alex Rodriguez**. I respect what Alex has accomplished and his credentials, but I'm leaving him off, I guess, for the performance-enhancing drug violations, and he also just did not strike me as a prototypical Yankee. He never did fit in with the organization and what it means to be in pinstripes.

Here is my batting order:
1. Derek Jeter
2. Don Mattingly
3. Mickey Mantle
4. Roger Maris
5. Yogi Berra
6. Scott Brosius
7. Roy White
8. Bobby Richardson
9. Whitey Ford(L)/"Catfish" Hunter (R)

The No. 6, 7, and 8 hitters will not wow you with their stats, but their ability to put the ball in play, to hit and run, or bunt when necessary makes them invaluable. And Bobby will get a lot of fastballs to hit batting in front of the pitcher. That's right, I said "pitcher." No designated hitter as long as I'm calling the shots. If we are going to play for the survival of the free world, I want to play "real" baseball. I don't know about you, but I'm already feeling pretty bad for the aliens.

CHAPTER 5
THE HOUSE(S) THAT RUTH BUILT

"We're relying on you to take the memories from this stadium and add them to the new memories that come to the new Yankee Stadium and continue to pass them on from generation to generation."

—*Derek Jeter*
September 21, 2008

Those are the words Yankees captain Derek Jeter said to a teary-eyed crowd after the final out of the final game at the old Yankee Stadium. For those who were there, it was a bittersweet moment. The old stadium was a concrete connection to the legends of the past. It was where many of their favorite Yankees memories were made. During the lifespan of the original "House That Ruth Built" from the inaugural game on April 18, 1923 (a victory over the rival Boston Red Sox) to Jeter's poignant words from the infield, more than 151 million people passed through the turnstiles of Yankee Stadium. That's a lot of memories. Through the years there have been some changes to the structure, the team's fortunes ebbed and flowed, great stars climbed and fell, legendary coaches came and went…and often came back again. But the stadium was always a constant year to year.

I myself have collected some pretty good Yankees memories. As a major league pitcher from the late 1950s to the early '80s—including a year in the Bronx—and an announcer in the '80s, '90s, and 2000s, I experienced plenty of moments that have been etched into my memory bank. I remember David Wells taking a few off-duty policemen down to the cages to throw them some batting practice the day of his perfect game. I remember sitting in the bullpen back in the '70s and seeing our coach—the legendary Elston Howard—sniff the air and say, "Ooh… they are smoking that stuff again" because the left-field stands out by the bullpen were a popular place for the pot smokers back then. And I'll never forget the chills of hearing Daniel Rodriguez sing "God Bless America" at the first game at the stadium after 9/11. I've heard stories and been a part of incidents that give me a unique perspective on this world-class organization.

When Yankee Stadium first opened in 1923, it was baseball's first triple-decker structure and the first ballpark to be labeled a "stadium." It came with an advertised capacity of 70,000, but that included a lot of folks standing out past the outfield fences. And there were only 16 bathrooms—eight men's rooms and eight women's restrooms. That's it. When the stadium was remodeled in the '70s, the bathrooms had risen to 50. The original field favored left-handed power hitters like Babe Ruth because of the short right-field foul pole sitting at a mouthwatering 295 feet from home plate. By the time you reached right-center field, the distance to hit a home run had ballooned to 429. For Lou Gehrig and the right-handed hitters, the left-field pole came in at 281 feet from the plate. It worked its way to 395 in left and to 460 in left-center field. And center field was a ridiculous 490 feet straight away. In the dead ball era, it might as well been located on the moon. The stadium had its first major alteration in 1937, when the wooden bleachers were replaced with concrete ones. But more importantly, the center-field fence was brought in to a still absurdly long 461. That was basically the Yankee Stadium I played in when I came up with the Washington Senators in 1959.

My first memory of Yankee Stadium was from the air. Growing up in Zeeland, Michigan, my main connection to the big leagues was the radio. But every year my dad would get the baseball guides from *Spalding's* and then *The Sporting News*. (I still have them, dating back to 1900.) Besides being full of every stat on every player who played the year before, it included a picture of every stadium in the majors. The pictures were usually from the air, so that was my frame of reference for Yankee Stadium.

Build Me a Home The original Yankee Stadium opened in 1923. The season ended with Babe Ruth leading the Bombers to their first World Series title, beating their cross-river rivals, the New York Giants, in six games. Fifty-three years later and after spending two seasons sharing Shea Stadium with the Mets, the Yankees returned to the stadium after a renovation project completed in 1976. That season also ended with the Yankees in the World Series, though this time they were swept by the Cincinnati Reds. The Yankees would claim back-to-back championships in '77 and '78. Fast forward to 2009, and they took over their new stadium. And once again, they made it to October, beating the Philadelphia Phillies in six games to claim their 27th World Series title.

At the end of 1959, I was called up by the Senators, and in September we played the Yankees. I was flying into LaGuardia Airport (that would later become JFK), and as we came in low over the Bronx, I saw the beautiful concrete horseshoe surrounding an emerald field. You couldn't miss it. Even at a few thousand feet of elevation, it really jumped out at you. Once I got to the stadium, I was in for another treat. There's something special about your first time at those old, historic ballparks. Fenway Park and Wrigley Field are the only ones left now. But you'd walk in at ground level under the grandstand and then go up a slight incline to get into the lower stands, and that's where the field came into view. There is nothing quite like that sight for baseball fan—or player for that matter—as you walk up that ramp. There is no grass greener or uniforms whiter than the first time you walk up that ramp into a big league ballpark.

Another thing that jumped out at you at the old Yankee Stadium was the monuments in center field. In 1932 the Yankees created their first memorial monument, and that was for manager Miller Huggins. But whoever thought it would be a good idea to put stone pillars with plaques to legendary players like Babe Ruth, Lou Gehrig, and Huggins in the field of play definitely never had to chase a ball bouncing around those tombstone-looking tributes. Comedian and lifelong Yankees fan Billy Crystal said he used to think those guys were buried out there. And there was a lot of "there" out there because of the expansive outfield. I am well-acquainted with that vast past space. I once watched a ball hit by Mickey Mantle off of me with two out in the bottom of the ninth inning clear the wall in 1967.

The place also sounded different. Back then, the speakers were at ground level so you could hear the announcements clearly in the bullpen or the dugout. I'll never forget hearing the voice of public address announcer Bob Sheppard for the first time. Bob began his Yankees career back in '51, the only season that Joe DiMaggio and Mantle shared the outfield. He would also announce New York Giants football games as well as baseball and football games at his alma mater, St. Johns University. A speech teacher by trade, Bob worked over 4, 500 Yankees games before retiring in 2007. And somehow his voice never changed. You'll never forget hearing…

> *Now batting for the Yankees*
> *No. 7…Mickey Mantle…*
> *No. 7*

In 2014 you could still hear Bob's recorded voice at the stadium. Younger fans know him as the voice that introduced Derek Jeter. And you can see the microphone he used for his first 50 seasons at Yankee Stadium at the Baseball Hall of Fame in Cooperstown. Bob was a part of 22 pennants and 13 championships. He earned both a World Series and a Super Bowl ring. No athlete in world can say that. May 7th, 2000, was "Bob Sheppard Day" at Yankee Stadium, and they unveiled his plaque in Monument Park. Bob is also probably the only person in the Yankees organization whom notorious micro-manager George Steinbrenner never tried change in any way. In all their time together, Bob never got a single note from George about his performance.

Bob's distinctive voice is one of the great connective threads in Yankees history. So many people try to imitate or impersonate it. Every announcer I know who's ever sat at a booth in Yankee Stadium at some point pretends to be Bob for a minute and introduces their favorite player into their headset. The media dining room in the new stadium is even named "Sheppard's Place." But no one could really replicate his style. Bob always said he tried to do three things: be clear, concise, and correct.

Sheppard passed away in 2010 at the age of 99—two days before another Yankees legend, George Steinbrenner, died. With his passing the Yankees not only lost a major part of their history, but baseball also lost one of its great treasures. Even the dreaded Boston Red Sox knew how special Bob was. No one less than the great Carl Yaztrzemski said, "You're not in the big leagues until Bob Sheppard announces your name."

Clubhouse Confidential

When I sat in the visiting clubhouse for my first game at Yankee Stadium, I realized it hadn't changed all that much from the Murderer's Row era. I could easily visualize my heroes—Boston's Ted Williams and Jimmie Foxx or the great Philadelphia A's pitcher Bobby Shantz—suiting up for a game there. All of a sudden, I am dressing in the same locker room they did. It was quite a thrill for this Midwestern kid. Fast forward to 2002, and I'm in the booth for the Yankees, and John Vander Wal is traded to New York from the San Francisco Giants. John hailed from Hudsonville, Michigan, which is only about 15 miles down the road from where I grew up in Zeeland. He'd spent his entire 11-year career up to that point in the National League. He was good with a bat. In fact he still holds the major league record for pinch-hits in a season, collecting 28 for the Colorado Rockies in 1995. So when he joined the Yankees, I was eager to hear this other Midwestern boy's reaction to playing in Boston's iconic Fenway Park for the first time. We were standing in front of the third-base dugout in Boston when I asked him, "What do you think, John?" He paused, then said, "Boy, it's pretty old. The clubhouse is pretty cramped." In that moment I saw a big generational gap in ballplayers.

Sure, I would've welcomed a little more comfort in the clubhouse in my day, but now there are also a lot more things to distract a player. For starters the TV is on in the locker room 24/7. When I played for the St. Louis Cardinals in the '80s, manager Whitey Herzog took the TV and postgame food out of our clubhouse. All we did was talk and think baseball. We ended up winning the World Series in 1982. Now it seems few players take the time to look at the history of these great old parks. It's *only* about the comfort factor and it's one of the big differences between the old and new-school players.

The other big change to come to clubhouses is the addition of female reporters. Back when I started my major league career, you'd never find a woman in the clubhouse during working hours. It was only men down there and in all of sports. Then women started knocking on the door. The great Lesley Visser, who is a good friend and is well thought of and has had a long, successful career, really helped pave the way. One of her first press credentials had her picture and name on the front and the words "No Women or Children in the Press Box" on the back. But Lesley really knew her stuff. Andrea Kirby was another. She was one of the—if not the first—on-air female sportscasters back in the early '70s for a local station in Florida. She would later coach me and several others in broadcast techniques during my ESPN days in the late '80s. It was not an easy road for women. I remember when a female reporter walked into our Philadelphia Phillies clubhouse back in the '70s. As she passed some of the players' wives, you heard a lot of nasty comments from them. And it was awkward in the early days until robes and interview rooms and players' lounges came into widespread use.

As far as I'm concerned, I don't care if a reporter is a man or a woman, as long as they know their topic. It's when you take someone who has never played or studied the game and you entrust them with commenting on it like they have played. That's when I have a problem. Of course, a male reporter with no knowledge of the game would be pretty much ignored by the players and have little chance of holding the job or even getting it in the first place. But a young, attractive female reporter will probably still land the interview. I know when I was a young, testosterone-filled lad it was very appealing to be asked to do an interview by an attractive female. Sure, there are ladies on TV who know absolutely nothing about what they are asked to comment on. But there are also women like Sam Ryan on MLB Network who work really hard and have a lot of inside stories that we use during games. A lot of times players will open up or be more relaxed talking to female reporters. I found that out when I was doing reports for David Hartman on *Good Morning America* in the mid '80s. It was often difficult to get a player to talk to me ahead of talking to an attractive female reporter. Fair or not, that's the way it goes. There is also the obvious side effect of having young, fit, people of the opposite sex in that often emotionally charged environment of the locker room. Late in the 2014 season, NESN reporter Jenny Dell—a first-class young lady—resigned from her position covering the Red Sox because she began dating Boston third baseman Will Middlebrooks. And both she and the team decided—in order to avoid any awkward situations— she would cover other things for NESN. There are other examples of that happening, but nobody should be surprised. Men are still men, and women are still women.

As a former player turned announcer, part of my job was to talk to the players before games and get some information I could relate to the fans during the broadcast. The ideal player to talk to—no surprise here—was Derek Jeter. He was always accessible, would answer just about any question but didn't want you sticking around making small talk. Paul O'Neill was another one. The Yankees, in general, in the mid-to-late '90s were as good as it gets for accessibility. Usually, if guys don't want to talk to you because they had a bad day, they'd go hide in the training room to avoid the media but not these guys. David Cone, Chuck Knoblauch, Bernie Williams—they were always very accessible and a treat to be around. When things changed for the Yankees, at least from my point of view, was when they started to bring in guys like Kevin Brown, Randy Johnson, and Mike Mussina. They'd often pass it off as being shy, but they were actually aloof, moody, and worried you'd ask a question they didn't want to answer—even if that was your job. They just were not as pleasant to deal with as the Yankees of the late '90s. It bears repeating, though, how pleasant Hideki Matsui was. Through his interpreter he was always there to answer questions. Alex Rodriguez was easy to talk to, but he always seemed very calculated. He wanted to be perceived as a nice guy and wanted to be liked. I just could never shake the feeling that what he said was less than 100 percent genuine.

Pinstripes and Disco Balls

In January of 1973, George Steinbrenner bought the Yankees from CBS for $10 million. At the end of the season and after 50 years of memories, Yankee Stadium was closed for major renovations. While the team played the next two seasons at Shea Stadium, the field was lowered several feet, and the lower seats were given more of a slope to improve visibility. Some creative engineering allowed them to remove many of the metal girders that held up the upper decks to improve sight lines. The iconic 15-foot-tall metal frieze that ringed the stadium was taken down before it fell on somebody. But it was such a part of the look of the stadium that they put a replica out across the top of the scoreboard in center. The dimensions changed, too. The center-field wall was brought in some forty feet to 417, so that the monuments were no longer in the field of play and were instead in the newly created Monument Park. They also added the first television screen in major league history to show replays of the action to fans during the game. The total price of the renovations was $160 million. Say what you will about Steinbrenner—and we will say a lot in Chapter 8—but George always wanted the best for Yankees fans. This was the stadium where the Yankees won back-to-back titles in the late '70s. It's also where I played parts of two seasons as a Yankee. That was definitely an interesting time to be in New York.

I had finally gotten to the point in my career and in my life where I could actually enjoy the Big Apple. As a 20-year-old kid coming up, I didn't dare get on the subway. I thought I might get lost and that they would never find me again. As they say, it's easier to take the boy out of the country, than the country out of the boy. I wouldn't even take the subway to the ballpark. But after coming to New York City for almost 20 years as a visiting player, I was finally comfortable enough to get on the subway in 1979. That really opened up the city to me. I was with the club right after their two championship seasons of '77, '78. It was really a special privilege to be in uniform as a New York Yankee. There were just so many perks around the city.

Joey D'Ambrosio, our public relations man, once came into the clubhouse and said, "We need somebody to attend Marvin Hamlisch's birthday party. His partner, Carole Bayer Sager, is throwing a birthday party for him, and he's such a big Yankees fan that he wants somebody in attendance." Well, I was living in midtown in an apartment I subletted on 59th and Central Park West. Marvin's apartment was over on Park Avenue, so I said I'd go. Marvin had won three Oscars in 1973 in a single night for his work on the music for two of the biggest movies of the decade—*The Sting* with Paul Newman and Robert Redford and *The Way We Were* with Barbra Streisand and Redford again. He'd also won a bunch of Grammys and co-wrote the theme song with his girlfriend, Carole, for the James Bond movie, *The Spy Who Loved Me*. He was a big, big deal. But I didn't know Marvin Hamlisch from Tom Thumb. I wasn't into the music world that much. I just thought it was a party near my apartment, so why not go?

So I walk in, and one of the first guys I run into is legendary entertainer Peter Allen. There were also Lucie Arnaz, Robert Klein, and, of course, Marvin and Carole—a star in her own right. Peter Allen broke out singing some of his famous songs like "I Could Have Been a Sailor" and "I Go to Rio." He ended up becoming one of my favorite entertainers. So that was pretty heady stuff for a kid from Zeeland, Michigan. As the years went on, I would see Marvin, and he'd introduce me, saying, "Oh, yeah, Jim was at my 35th birthday." Before he passed away in 2012, Marvin became one of just two people to achieve the "grand slam-plus" of entertainment awards, winning a Pulitzer Prize, an Emmy, a Grammy, an Oscar, and a Tony. (The other was the great composer Richard Rodgers of Rodgers and Hammerstein fame.) Marvin was such a great talent.

I was never a big-city lights kinda guy, but Studio 54 was in its heyday when I was with the Yankees. There was the famous sports bar on the upper east side of Manhattan called Oren and Aretsky's. I used to go there a lot. It was owned by Kenny Aretsky and Steve Orenstein, and a lot of jocks and models frequented the joint. The owners both knew Mark Benecke, the famous doorman at Studio 54, who was a huge Yankees fan. So any time friends or players from other teams came to town, I suddenly became their Studio 54 tour guide.

I'll never forget the World Series of '81. I was no longer with the Yankees then, having been sold to the St. Louis Cardinals in 1980, but the Yankees were back in the Fall Classic. At this point I had played in a World Series back in '65 when the Minnesota Twins lost to the Los Angeles Dodgers in seven games. But this was the first World Series game I attended as a fan. Heck, it might have been one of the first big league games I went to as an adult without being in uniform. I went with my good buddy from my Philly days, Tim McCarver, and a mutual friend, Tom Richmond. After Game 1 the three of us hitched a ride in a limo with Dick Enberg, the legendary announcer who was there for the World Series, and the topic of Studio 54 came up. Dick said, "Wow, I wonder if we could get in there."

I said, "You all want to go? I can get you into Studio 54." They couldn't believe it. It was one of the hardest places to get into in the entire city. "Don't worry, fellas," I said. "I know a guy." That "guy," of course, was the doorman, Mark. We got there, and the line to get in went up and down the block. We walked over to the side door, said a few words to Mark, he lifted the velvet rope, and we were in. I really felt like, as the kids say, a "playa" that night. Inside it was like everything you read about—people in wild costumes, shirtless busboys, a giant moon with a cocaine spoon hanging over the dance floor, and no holds barred. People were doing drugs at the tables or getting busy just right out there in the open. It was the wildest nightclub you could imagine. Here we were dressed like normal guys in slacks and sport coats and we looked kind of out of place in there. So we grabbed a corner and did some great people watching. You'd see the best soccer player in the world, Pelé, who played for the New York Cosmos soccer team, and the famous model and actress Margaux Hemingway. But what really caught your eye were all the regular people there who left their inhibitions outside with Mark the doorman. It was really a freak show and quite an experience even in New York City.

Because of the significance of the franchise in that city, that's the kinds of thing you were exposed to as a member of the Yankees. That was something totally new to me. Even though I had played in the big leagues for two decades by that point and played on some good teams, I never received the kind of recognition that you got as a member of the Yankees. Even putting on the pinstripes, it was different. I got traded from the Twins to the Chicago White Sox, for whom I wore a powder blue uniform with red shoes on the road. I felt like a clown. And then with the Phillies, we also had powder blue uniforms. Well, now, with the Yankees, I was back to the traditional pinstripes with no name on the back and black shoes. I felt like I was sort of an old-time ballplayer again because that's the way it was when I came up, and that's the way it's always been with the Yankees. And, of course, there were all the hair rules of Steinbrenner's. You couldn't have a beard, and your hair had to be a certain length. There's nothing wrong with having personal taste and the freedom to wear your hair and do what you want, but I liked the way we had to dress and look back in the day, and the Yankees have maintained that. It gives a team a much more professional look.

Field of Dreams...or Nightmares?

The new Yankee Stadium opened in 2009. It is the third largest and third youngest stadium in the majors. I'm sure plenty of fans love the new place, but if you ask me, I'm not a fan—at least not yet. I know what they were going for when they built it: to combine the modern amenities of stadiums of today and the dimensions and look of the old Yankee Stadium. And that makes sense. Fans like the wide concourses and escalators. There are tons of great food choices, as long as you don't mind paying $6 for a hot dog. The seats are more comfy. Many of the views are better, though some seats out in right-center field have to come with TVs in order for you to see more than one-third of the field.

But to me, the playing field is a disaster. It's like making a little league park out of Yankee Stadium. Balls go over the fence in right-center field so easily it's a joke. Johnny Damon was a heck of a player, but when a guy with his power starts hitting like 25 home runs a year, there is something wrong. They don't even have a number out there to tell you what the actual dimensions are. Yankee Stadium was always known for having short porches down the lines. But as a pitcher you knew that if you could keep ball in the middle of the field from right-center to left-center, you had a chance to keep it in the park. Left-center field at the old stadium was known as Death Valley. Get a hitter to hit it there, and it was usually a fly out. Now in right-center field, they don't even measure it. Balls just fly over that wagon gate, hour after hour. Makes you wonder what Ruth would have hit there? Or Mantle? Or DiMaggio?

147

Another aspect of the new stadium is the loss of the 10th man. Many times in the old stadium, I would feel the place shake when the fans really got going. That doesn't seem to be the case in the new place. Mariano Rivera even said in his book, *The Closer*, that the new stadium "doesn't hold noise or home-team fervor anywhere near the way the old place did." It definitely worked well enough for Mariano and the boys to win a championship their first season in the place, but I know what he's saying. Maybe that will change over time. Maybe, like me, he looks back at the old days with rose-colored contacts. I just feel like the game is more artificial in the stadium today than in the original. I'll always like the flavor and the dimension of the original. Of course, if you put in those dimensions (457 to left-center), you'd have hitters and their agents calling and complaining to the Yankees because they want their clients to hit home runs. And they are a lot harder to hit when the wall is 457 feet away.

But if they had taken more of the dimensions of the old "House That Ruth Built" stadium from the '60s and captured more of the old-time architecture, it would've been a really special ballpark. Instead you have something that some people call "The House That *Ruthless* Men Built," implying a desire to favor the almighty dollar over the traditions of our National Pastime. I'm sure another 85 years from now when they are opening Yankee Stadium IV and our "new" version has become the "old" one, someone will be looking back fondly at this stadium, recalling how the grass was greener and the uniforms whiter. I wonder what a hot dog will cost then?

I'm sure some of you who love the new ballpark aren't too happy with what I think. Well, if you know anything about me, you know that's what I do. I tell you what I think. I always have. That doesn't mean it's right or wrong. But I have found that, even though it rubs the occasional feather the wrong way, it's the best way to be in my business. I didn't arrive to that conclusion all by myself. No sir. I had plenty of help getting from the field to the booth and learning to stick to my convictions along the way.

CHAPTER 6

GETTING THERE

It's September 16, 2006. I am standing on the mound at Yankee Stadium. The stands are full. The Yankees are about to take on the Boston Red Sox. I've stood on this mound plenty of times before—both in pinstripes and as a member of the visiting team. I pitched my very first major league victory on this bump way back in 1960. But this was the one and only time I was out there where I was flanked by three of my grandkids.

After nearly 1,500 games spread out across a dozen years in three different decades on three different networks, I was retiring as a Yankees broadcaster. During my tenure I was fortunate to have seen their runs to four World Series titles as well as two additional American League pennants. But if you added up all my time in the game from little league to this point, the baseball miles on my 67-year-old chassis would number in the millions. It was time to hang up my microphone. Actually it was slightly *past* that time—24 hours past to be exact.

If everything had gone according to plan, I would've retired on the 15th. That's when I was scheduled to call my last game for the YES Network. Sitting alongside my boothmate, Bobby Murcer, I was to say good-bye to all the fans who took me into their homes over the years. But Mother Nature had other plans, I guess, because she rained out the game. It was to be made up the next day as a doubleheader. No big deal. That happens all the time. But that doubleheader would be on FOX, not YES, so I wasn't going to work the game. In truth, it didn't bother me any. I'm not the sentimental type. After all, fans come to the games for the players, not the announcers. So I made some arrangements to record a special farewell to the fans. I said good-bye to all of my great co-workers on the production team, the ones who made me look and sound better than any announcer has the right to look or sound for all those years. And I was about to head off into retirement—when George Steinbrenner's office called.

Yankees marketing director Debbie Tymon told me that George

wanted to know if I'd come back the next night to throw out the first pitch. It was an awfully nice gesture and very much in character for George. I, of course, accepted. So there I am, in golf shirt and jeans, watching a video tribute they had made for me playing on the Jumbotron. I won't lie; it was a pretty special moment, seeing that with my daughter and grandkids there with me, hearing the crowd's reactions. Red Sox manager Terry Francona—"Tito"—even had all of the Red Sox standing on the top step of the dugout. Then, with my special guests miming along, I threw out the first pitch. Yankees reliever Mike Myers caught it. I shook hands with Joe Torre and Tito and then headed up to the booth. On top of George's offer, FOX had asked if I'd like to call an inning of the game to say my farewell to the Yankees fans. It was another kind gesture that I humbly accepted. I got to the booth and took my spot next to Josh Lewin and Tim McCarver. Again, I am not a sentimental man by nature, but there was something special about calling my last Yankees game sitting next to Tim. Because of all the fine people over the years who had a hand in me becoming an announcer, you would find more of Tim's fingerprints on the finished product than anyone else's. Although he was perhaps the man most responsible for my long tenure as an announcer, he wasn't the man who put that crazy idea in my head. That honor goes to a different iconic broadcaster.

Stepping Up to the Mic

"You know you can't play forever. What are you going to do *after* baseball?" That was the question put to me during a pregame interview in 1964 by the great Ray Scott. Ray was the longtime voice of the Green Bay Packers. He also covered the Minnesota Twins. Scott was known for his famous call: "Starr…Dowler…touchdown." I had listened to him countless times growing up, and if there is a man who can say more with less, I've never met him. So here I was, all of 25 years old,

As part of my farewell announcing Yankees games, I throw out the first pitch on September 16, 2006, while being flanked by three of my grandkids. *(AP Images)*

talking to a broadcast legend, when I hear myself say, "Kinda looks like fun, doing what you're doing." As I look back now, I realize my answer was more knee-jerk reaction than carefully thought out career planning. But it turned out to be right on the money.

The next day the Twins got a call from a man named Bob Zellner. He had heard what I had said with Scott and he offered me a job on his radio station when the season ended. So that fall, I started at KSMM— "Kissem, the voice of the Progress Valley!"—a 500-watt daytime station in Shakopee, Minnesota. For someone who was interested in broadcasting—or at least had said on the air that he was interested in broadcasting—it was a great training ground because I did *everything*. I came on with the national anthem and did news, weather, sports, and, of course, the all-important livestock reports. For all of you young wannabe announcers out there, just remember before you can talk about the finer points of Mariano Rivera's splitter, you have to update the public on a few Hereford sales. I remember driving into work in the wee hours of the morning when it was 20 below zero outside. I'd be screaming inside my car trying to warm my voice up so it would be clear on air. The next year I moved up to the bigger KRSI and did a variety of sports shows, but my radio days didn't progress much past that at the time. A man can only scream at so many windshields before he starts questioning his sanity.

I guess the next step in my training for the booth came later in my career, when I was with Philadelphia from 1976 to '79. During rain delays Phillies announcers Richie Ashburn and Harry Kalas would ask for a player to come up to the booth and chat to fill the time. By then I had been in the league almost 20 years so I was frequently requested. It gave me a fair share of practice in front of the microphone. But in truth the best training I got in Philadelphia was in the dugout because that's where I got to know Tim McCarver. And I am not exaggerating when I say I believe Tim singlehandedly changed the way the game is called today.

Considering how close we are now, I have to laugh when I think back on our first meeting. It did not go so well. It came in spring training. I think I was playing for the Chicago White Sox at the time, and Tim was catching for the Phillies. I was coming up to hit, and my competitive nature got the best of me. Tim had gotten a broken-bat hit on me, and when I stepped in the batter's box, I kidded him about it. I must've said something snide, something Tim didn't take too kindly to. As far as he was concerned, we were not meant to ever be friends. But once we became teammates in Philly, we realized we watched the game the same way. Before you know it, we were playing bridge and eating dinner together. In no time we were very good friends.

By this time in his career, Tim only caught Steve Carlton, which means he played once every three or four days. So we got to sit on the bench together and observe what was really happening on the field. Little did we know it at that time, but it was prepping us for broadcasting. While everyone else was looking where the ball went, we looked inside of that. Tim would notice when a left fielder was not playing shallow enough with a left-handed hitter in the batter's box. He knew when a lefty hits it that way, it's off the end of the bat, and it doesn't go as far. He was on top of little things like that. Unless you played the game or had been there, you just can't bring that kind of analysis to the game. Tim was a master at that.

Tim started his broadcasting career in 1980 with the Phillies, then went to the New York Mets, and then on to a terrific career working the biggest games for most networks. After all his years analyzing World Series and postseason play, Tim really earned the reputation for taking the fans inside the game. Although I'm a big proponent of the inside game, the two biggest things I learned from Timmy were to be honest and objective. And there is no one I know more brutally honest and objective than Tim McCarver. He has that very rare quality where he does not mind telling you how he feels even if it might hurt your feelings.

But if you are worth your salt, it doesn't hurt your feelings because he's being completely honest.

Here's an example of Tim's fearless honesty. In his early days as a Philly broadcaster, our teammate and very good friend, Mike Schmidt, hit a ball to left-center that he thought was going to be a home run and he broke into a trot. But the ball stayed in, and the outfield threw to second and kept Schmitty to a single. Tim immediately said that Mike should've been on second, that he wasn't running hard on that ball. But then he backed it up with a reason. Tim said, "What often happens with home run hitters—they can tell by the sound of the ball hitting the bat whether it's going out of the park or not, and they are usually right. So they automatically go into their trot and sometimes they get caught looking like they didn't run hard."

The next day Schmidt pulled Tim aside. "I heard you said I wasn't running hard."

Tim responded, "That's right you weren't. And then I explained why." That was pure Tim—honest and objective. And I consider myself very fortunate that I got to learn firsthand how important those two qualities are for an analyst.

With all the technology now, the fan doesn't just need a funny story and a few stats. They are overwhelmed with stats. They need someone to tell them what they can't read in the paper or see graphically like what is the manager thinking, what's going on between the pitcher and catcher, why are they playing this guy to pull, why put in *this* pitcher in the eighth? Tim was the pioneer in giving us all those angles to talk about while making the game entertaining for the fans. We all owe him—and me in particular—a big token of gratitude.

I got more experience in the booth during the players' strike of 1981. I ended up calling some minor league games for the Baltimore Orioles with the great Ralph Kiner and Warner Fusselle. From that I put together a tape of my work and sent it around. Next thing I know, I was hired by ESPN to do some early-round games in the College World Series. Brent Musburger was there to do final games for CBS, but he heard me on a few of my broadcasts and told Ted Shaker at CBS, "If you guys ever get baseball, give this Jim Kaat guy a good look." (Ted eventually did hire me in 1990, and I owe both men a debt of gratitude for helping my career along.)

My last year in the majors was 1983. After 20-plus seasons and 283 wins and one World Series ring, I was unceremoniously let go by the St. Louis Cardinals. (Thank goodness I'm not sentimental.) In that transition from player to former player, the two most obvious career paths are coaching and broadcasting. As I was trying to figure out my next move, I received a call from NBC. In 1984 NBC had the rights to the *MLB Game of the Week* and often did doubleheaders on the weekends. Yankees great Tony Kubek would be the color analyst for the A-game, and I got to do the B-game. This brought me into contact with some great play-by-play announcers like Dick Enberg, Dick Stockton, and Greg Gumbel. They taught me how to take all those things I used to notice in the dugout with McCarver and work them into a TV broadcast, how to get my thoughts in, and then get out of the way so the director can do his thing. It's a complicated dance with so many moving parts. When it's all working together, you never notice it.

Later during the 1984 season, Pete Rose called and asked me to be his pitching coach in Cincinnati. I took the job out of respect for Pete asking me and out of curiosity to see if what I learned from coaches would be helpful to me as a coach. (It was.) So I became a Red. And I enjoyed coaching, but the financial compensation for the time commitment was less than ideal, and the short contracts offered little stability. When I couldn't get a three-year contract from the Reds in 1985, I decided to turn in my coaching cap and return to broadcasting.

A Booth in the Bronx

My Yankees broadcasting career began innocently enough in a Sarabeth's restaurant on Manhattan's Upper West Side in the fall of 1985. I had decided to start pursuing announcing jobs in the offseason and I took an apartment in the city to try and make contacts. So I was reading the *New York Post* that morning when I saw that the Yankees were looking for someone to replace Frank Messer, who was relieved of his duties as announcer after 18 years. Unfortunately, that was no surprise during the George Steinbrenner Era. I was all too familiar with it, having played for the Yankees in '79 and '80. Still, I was here looking for broadcasting jobs, and here was one of the best in the world staring me in the face.

I called the Yankees and talked to a guy in public relations named Joe D'Ambrosio. He surprised me when he said, "I'm glad you called. The producer Don Carney has been trying to reach you." I couldn't believe it. *They were looking for me to announce Yankees games?* Apparently, Don remembered those rain delay interviews I did with the Phillies. Before I knew it, I was meeting Leavitt Pope, who ran the station at WPIX. I didn't have a tape of my work, but he said, "I don't need a tape. I know what you can do. I just have to get this approved by George."

I had a run-in with Mr. Steinbrenner when I played for him. A disingenuous negotiation in 1980—where he claimed to have forgotten the conversation in which we agreed to terms—led to me being shipped off to St. Louis. In all, I had spent less than a year in New York, but before I left, I fired off some angry letters and I'm sure a few ended up on George's desk. I was fairly certain that those letters would come back to haunt me and sink my chances for the job. But apparently George forgot those letters—just like he forgot our verbal agreement—because he blessed my hiring. And my second Yankees career was off and running. Unfortunately it would last about as long as the first.

In 1986 I was just three years removed from my playing days and sharing a booth with two longtime broadcasting icons, Phil Rizzuto and

Bill White. "Scooter," as Rizzuto is known, was a much beloved Yankees fixture, and I certainly enjoyed working with him. And everyone who has worked with Rizzuto has a story—or 12—about him. But the best thing about my first tour of duty as a Yankees broadcaster was White. Bill was the very first African American to regularly do play-by-play for a major league team, and, though he was only five years older than I was at the time, I consider him my broadcast mentor as well as my very good friend. His advice was simple: speak your mind and stay true to you convictions. That's simple to say but not always to follow. Bill warned me that the Yankees brass would try and put words in my mouth. Steinbrenner would send notes to the booth, telling the announcers to say this or that. "Don't fall for it," Bill would say. Besides helping my career, Bill was pretty good at seeing where it was going. "You might only last a year here, Jim," he'd say, "because by management standards, you're not a 'true Yankee,' having only played parts of two seasons." Well, I followed Bill's advice and stuck to my convictions, and in the end, he was right—I was out after only the one season. Apparently, George didn't like some of the things I said that weren't pro-Yankee in his eyes.

So, in 1988 I went back to Minneapolis and worked for the Twins for the next six seasons. I also did weekend games for CBS, continued to hone my craft, and built on the basics that Tim instilled in me. And while Tim is the biggest influence on the kind of announcer I would become, it was Kubek who was responsible for where I found a home.

Tony was a beloved pinstriped icon. The Rookie of the Year in '57, he played in six World Series for the Yankees in nine years. Later as a broadcaster, he would call twice that many championships with NBC. If you are tracking the evolution of the baseball color commentator on TV from storyteller to expert analyst, then Kubek would have to be one of those all important missing links. In the early days of TV broadcasts, great players like Dizzy Dean and Pee Wee Reese were in the booth to tell amusing anecdotes about their playing days. They didn't take you

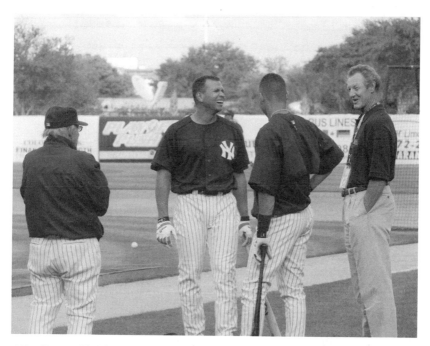

After George Steinbrenner greenlit my second announcing stint with the Yankees, I covered the team, including in spring training of 2004, when I visited with (from left to right) Yogi Berra, Alex Rodriguez, and Derek Jeter.

inside the game. Joe Garagiola was the same way. They were entertaining without a doubt; they just weren't educating the fan. Then along comes Kubek.

He approached the position from a fan's perspective. What would the guy sitting at home on the couch find interesting about the game? Tony started as a human-interest, sideline-type reporter but gradually moved to become an analyst and when he did—look out. He told it like he saw it. And he was fearless. When then-commissioner Bowie Kuhn missed the game where Hank Aaron hit his record-breaking 715th home run, Tony said he should have been there. He was the ultimate straight shooter and the biggest reason I landed with the Yankees.

Tony called Yankees games for the MSG Network for five seasons in the early '90s. But after the 1994 season with its labor issues, strike, and canceled World Series, Tony had had enough. He retired from broadcasting. (Tony even told *The New York Times* in 2008 that he hasn't seen a single major league baseball game since leaving the booth.) But before he left, he told MSG Network that the guy they should hire as his replacement was a tall left-handed former Yankees pitcher whom everyone called "Kitty." At the time I was working for ESPN. I was rollerblading down a street in Madison, Connecticut, with my late wife, MaryAnn, when I heard a voice call my name. And I'm thinking, *Who knows I'm here in Madison?* It was Bryan Burns, who was director of broadcasting for Major League Baseball. He said, "Mike McCarthy of MSG Network is trying to reach you. Kubek is going to retire and he recommended that they talk to you about the job." Tony was always kind to me. He is in the Broadcast Hall of Fame and will go down as one of the nice guys that all of us former players-turned-broadcasters trusted. He never hesitated to visit with us and let us pick his brain as we were learning the ropes about analyzing baseball on TV. But there was still one problem... Steinbrenner.

MSG wouldn't hire me without the Boss' blessing. Considering our track record, I figured I had two strikes against me. And I could see the third one coming in—high and hard. Instead I get a phone call from George. He mentioned MSG wanting to hire me, and our troubles were in the past. But there was something else that bothered George more than our run-ins. He said he had a terrible relationship with Kubek. It got to the point where they weren't even speaking. That wasn't a road George wanted to go down again. I told George, as far as I was concerned, the past was in the past. I would be there to cover the Yankees, not dredge up old disagreements. That was all he needed to hear.

CHAPTER 7
IN THE BOOTH

A microphone is a very powerful thing; it can both enlighten and entertain. It can relay information and opinions. A microphone can help you let everybody in on the joke or get you in trouble. Used wisely, it can change your view of the pictures that play out in front of you. Used poorly, it gets in the way of those same pictures and ruins the whole experience. I've been behind a microphone going on 34 years now, and I've seen, heard, and said just about everything you can imagine. But the microphone is a one-way street. And while most people have little problem letting us announcers into their living rooms through our microphones, they have no idea what our work environment is like. Sure, you might see us between innings once in a while during a game, but we know you're coming and we spruce up the place, kind of like when the in-laws come to town. In this chapter we'll pull away the curtain and give you a behind-the-scenes look at the inner workings of the major league broadcast booth.

Best Seat in the House?

I know a lot of people keep track of how many major league stadiums they've been to. They compare how the fields look, the sight lines. This one has more comfortable seats, but this one has great food, etc. Although they are all built to play baseball in, there are giant variations from stadium to stadium. The same is true for the press boxes. I've been in more than 50 of them during my broadcast days, including minor league and college. And in all of those, I'd have to say my favorite was the old Briggs Stadium, which became Tiger Stadium, in Detroit. I remember carrying on a conversation with former Minnesota Twins first baseman Kent Hrbek *while Herbie was in the on-deck circle*. You were that close. You could talk with players like you were in hotel lobby. And if a foul ball came straight back, you had to have your glove ready because it was not too far removed from the backstop. Ernie Harwell, the great Hall of

Fame announcer for the Tigers, had a net installed in front of him. If he was looking at his scorebook during a broadcast, he'd have some protection. But for the rest of us covering the game, we had to really be on our toes. Larry Osterman, who was the longtime Tigers radio announcer, was once knocked off his chair when a foul ball hit him in the chest. The old Comiskey Park had a small booth they used occasionally called "The Catbird Seat." It was similar in position to the Detroit booth, up close but with worse visibility. As risky as they were, I loved being that close to the action as an announcer. I was sad to see those booths go.

There are some good ones still out there. Camden Yards in Baltimore is nice and roomy. It had great crab cakes there back in the day but not anymore. Dodger Stadium, which is one of the oldest parks in the majors, is nice, neat, and clean, but the booths can be a little tight. Fenway is the toughest. The booth is way too high, and it is tough to get perspective on high fly balls. It's like watching from the top of the Prudential Center. Adding to that, it's very cramped up there. A counter and a couple of chairs—that's it. Listen to games at Fenway, and there will be a pause on high fly balls as the announcer tries to sort out where it's going.

The game has changed a lot over the years, and the stadiums have followed suit. For one thing the addition of luxury boxes usually means the broadcast booths have been moved farther away from the action. The other problem is just the sheer volume of entities covering any one game. Back in the old radio days when the Yankees went to play the Chicago White Sox, Yankees announcers stayed in New York and did the game by ticker tape. Someone in Chicago would be watching the game and typing the action in shorthand into a machine like a stock ticker. That would go over the wires to New York, where a machine there would print it out, and the announcers would call the action as if they were watching it, but they were just reading it off of the ticker tape.

When I started doing this for a living in the mid-1980s, you would usually have two TV broadcast booths, one for the home team and one for the visitors. The same would be true for radio, one for each. Nowadays, there can be six, seven, maybe more different broadcasts doing a single game. There is the home booth, the visiting booth, the Spanish language home, the Spanish language visitors, the Japanese language home, and Japanese language visitors. There might be FOX or one of the cable networks—ESPN, TBS, or MLB—covering games. So you need all this space for all these broadcasters, but the company that owns the team doesn't want to give up any real estate in the stadium to us announcers because that means fewer seats for them to sell. The end result is booths that are often crammed into very tight quarters. The home announcers are usually taken care of pretty well. I am now calling games for MLB Network, so I don't get those home booths anymore. That's why if you hear a longer than normal pause before I comment on a play, please be patient. There are probably times where you at home are closer to the action than I am in the broom closet-turned-broadcast booth down the first-base line.

The booth at Yankee Stadium had a row at the top of the booth for guests. In the MSG Network days, we could invite people to sit in the booth for a few innings and watch us work. We'd have dignitaries like mayor Rudy Giuliani or celebrities like Kevin Costner up there. When Joe Torre was back from his cancer surgery, we had Michael Milken promoting prostate cancer awareness. Hugh Jackman was there once. Then there was the time we had Bob Remus up in the booth. Back when I was first trying out radio back in the early '60s and I was on KSMM in Minnesota during the offseason, I would often cover high school football games. Chaska High School had a tremendous lineman named Bob Remus. Bob was All-Conference and Player of the Year. Well, some 20 odd years later, I ran into him in New York City, only by this time he was going by his professional name, Sergeant Slaughter. That's right; we had a professional wrestler up in the booth.

The Booth That Ruth Built

When I worked for New York, my office was the booth at the old Yankee Stadium, though it had been refurbished in the early '70s. I was in that old booth back in 1986 with WPIX and then again from 1994 through 2006 with MSG and the YES Network. I never worked in the home booth at the new stadium, but I've been in it.

We had a few TV monitors. One was called "network return." That showed what was going out over the air with that all important seven-second delay from our actual live announcing. When you are watching a live sporting event, it's not actually live. It is delayed seven seconds in the TV truck. That way if somebody slips up and drops one of George Carlin's "seven words you can't say on TV," a censor in the truck can hit a button and edit it out so it doesn't go out over the broadcast. We also had a telestrator monitor where we could draw telestrations and highlight something on a replay, so the viewer could understand it better. And there was a replay monitor where the truck could show us a replay before it was on the air, so analysts could get their thoughts together before talking about it on air. I also usually kept a pair of binoculars handy to see who was warming up in the bullpen or I'd use them to zoom in on the pitching mound to see if I could detect anything in the conversation between pitcher and catcher or pitching coach or manager on their visits.

We often had six to eight people in that booth during a broadcast. In addition to the two or three of us announcers, we'd always have a stage manager, who is the unsung hero of the telecast. The stage manager is the person who counts us in from commercial breaks so we know when we are on the air. They look at elements like pre-produced packages or graphics to make sure they are ready. They make sure we have everything we need or want as well as a few things we don't necessarily want but that we have to do—like promo cards. If something goes wrong, the stage manager is the first line of defense. Let's say my headset stops working

165

while we are on the air. The stage manager then alerts the production team to get someone to fix it, and they keep the info between truck and booth flowing. Without a stage manager, a lot more mistakes would make it on air. Audrey McLaughlin was our stage manager at Yankee Stadium. She was great. Robby Neilson is a fellow out west, and John Reynolds, "J.R.," often did Los Angeles Dodgers and Angels games.

Another body in the booth that is very important to the broadcast is the stats person. They support the announcers and frankly make the on-air talent sound way smarter than we probably are. The best stats guy I ever worked with was Mike Scheinkman. He's an attorney now, but, man, was he unbelievable at finding interesting facts really fast. The trick is not just knowing numbers and dates but knowing the right stat at the right time. When it is relevant? When does it help tell a story or add something to a game? Let's say Paul O'Neill hits a double. Mike would be on his computer and come back with a specific fact to put it into some historical perspective. Bob's son, Keith Costas, who works on MLB Network, is also very good at that. Another nationally known guy is Marty Aronoff. I haven't worked with Marty much, but he's a good friend. Bob Costas uses a guy named Eliott Kalb, who is so good they call him "Mr. Stats."

But times have changed even here. It used to be the stats person would find a stat and tell the graphics department. They would build the graphic and tell the technical director (whose position is discussed later) that it was ready to use when a particular batter stepped up to the plate. These days stats are often seamless in games. The graphic machines are connected directly to Elias Sports Bureau (or whatever stats company the particular network uses). So when Jacoby Ellsbury comes up to bat against Justin Verlander, the graphic that pops up on his average against this pitcher is accurate up to that second. But even with the technology, there is still plenty for the stats person to find. These people don't get mentioned too often, but they are a crucial part of the production team.

At home you hear the announcers, but there is a ton of chatter going on behind the scenes to make the broadcast happen. You have producers who are basically our managers. They are in charge of everything. They start working on games sometimes weeks in advance, making sure that everyone has everything they need to do the game justice. They work with everyone from the on-air talent to the director to the runners and interns. They are the ones steering the ship, and if the game suddenly goes off in a different direction, they are the ones who have to make sure that the team is all on the same page and pulling in the same direction. Leon Schweir was my producer back when I was with MSG Network. I learned a lot from him. Bob Dekas at CBS was another great one. Now I'm fortunate to work with Chris Pfeiffer on MLB Network. All of these guys are fantastic managers of the production team.

If producers are like managers, then the directors are like the pitching coaches. They control the cameras and replays and make sure that the action is covered the way the producer wants—much like a pitching coach gets the pitching staff to do what the manager wants. The technical director or TD helps the director do his job. Every time you see a camera angle change when you are watching the game, a lot is going on between the director, the technical director, and the cameramen. For a baseball game, there are usually eight or nine cameras covering the field. During the playoffs that'll go up to 15. And the World Series is even more than that. They all get fed into the truck and are on a wall full of monitors. The director watches them *all* at the same time. How do they do this? I don't know, but they do. That's how he tells the story of the game. When he wants to go from one camera to the next, he'll say, "Ready Camera Two, take Camera Two." On "take," the TD hits a button to switch what you are seeing at home from Camera Seven to Camera Two. And that goes on for every single camera change, and it happens hundreds of times per game. I've been fortunate to work with some great directors. John Moore on MLB Network is a super one. Bob Fishman on CBS is another fantastic one. I also had the pleasure working with the great Bill Webb on MSG Network. Bill is a legend and still out there doing his thing.

The camermen are another important part of that process. They don't get enough credit because tracking a hit baseball is a difficult thing. You have no idea where it's going, it's moving very fast, and it's pretty darn small. Somehow these guys and gals keep that three-inch diameter sphere in focus as it flies around the ballpark. And the real good ones notice things through their lenses that tell the story of the game. Maybe it's a pitcher changing his grip on the mound, or when MSG first-base cameraman Dave Chesney saw Rod Carew in the Angels dugout telling the Anaheim hitters that he'd figured out Andy Pettitte was tipping his pitches. They all deserve a lot of credit for doing a tough job and making it look easy. There is also a replay producer, who is looking at all the replays and telling the director and producer which ones are best and then cueing them up so the director can call for them and the TD can switch to them. That also goes on time and time again during a broadcast.

And then there are graphics. If you know anything about me, you know this is a sensitive subject with me. The guys and gals in graphics work really hard and have to keep up with an ever-changing game as well as all the technological bells and whistles. Some graphics, of course, are sponsored elements and those help pay the bills. I get that. And I know some of it is because the demographic of the viewer has changed. The XBox generation loves graphics. I just think graphics are way overdone these days. The great Dick Stockton used to say: "When a graphic goes up and I'm a fan, I want to say, 'Wow, I didn't know that.'" In my opinion that's a rare occurrence nowadays.

The definition of a perfect graphic for me came during Game 5 of the 1985 NLCS between the St. Louis Cardinals and the Los Angeles Dodgers. The score was tied 2–2 in the bottom of the ninth inning as Ozzie Smith, all 5'10", 150 pounds of him, steps in to face

6'5" hard-throwing right-hander, Tom Niedenfuer. The switch-hitting Smith was batting from the left side. He wasn't known for home run power, but the graphic that came up read: "Never hit a home run as a left-handed hitter in his career." That was something I didn't know. So what does Ozzie do: he hits a home run from the left side to win the game! (That was the hit that inspired Jack Buck's famous call: "Go crazy, folks! Go crazy!") That graphic added to the drama of the moment. The fact that I still remember it to this day says it had that "wow" factor.

Many of the graphics these days, I feel, are meaningless. One play can quickly move the team batting average or team ERA up or down. (The Red Sox team ERA during the Pedro Martinez period was low because Pedro was the lowest in the league.) My least favorite is average runs scored. Let's say the Yankees are averaging six runs a game. That sounds good, but they won 10–2 and 9–4 and they lost 3–2 and 4–3. So they scored 24 runs in four games, but they're 2–2. Big deal. One that I do like and do my best to promote is the swing run, which "swings" a team from winning to losing most of the time. It is the run a team has to score to be consistently at or over .500. For the past 25 years, that number has been four for most teams. For some squads with exceptional pitching—like the 1990s Atlanta Braves—it is three.

Another stat I find useful is the quality start. Some people scoff at the term, which was introduced by a terrific writer from Detroit named John Lowe back in the late '80s. It is called a quality start if the pitcher pitches six innings and allows three earned runs or less. The first reaction if you follow the game closely is: "That's an ERA of 4.50. That's not really that good." But that's forgetting the "or less" factor in the quality start. Over the past 26 years, my friend and personal pitching stat expert, Merrianna McCully, can show that the average ERA in a quality start game is a little over 2.00 in the American League and a little under 2.00 in the National League. If you get a quality start from your starters, you will win 65 to 70 percent of your games, and that probably means a pennant. These are examples of how just throwing a graphic out there without being able to explain it doesn't help the game, in my opinion.

One question that I'm asked a lot is, "Do announcers eat during the games?" I don't. I drink coffee or water, but I very rarely eat. But some guys are voracious eaters. Paul O'Neill comes to mind. Despite being as fit as he is, he will just devour large quantities of food. When I eat too much, I get sleepy. And in these days of the three to three-and-a-half hour game, you need to do all you can to stay awake and stay energized. That is the biggest challenge actually, keeping your energy for a long blowout. Sometimes you can sense when your partner has lost their spark. (I'm sure some have caught me as well,) and then it becomes more work than fun.

Aside from food, another broadcasting question I often get is about the Call of Nature. One of the first things I do when I get to the booth at a stadium is find the location of the nearest men's room. I've had to make more than a few sprints down a concourse during a commercial break because I don't think an umpire is gonna delay the start of the seventh inning of a late September Yankees-Red Sox game just because ol' Jim Kaat drank a little too much water in the fifth.

The final question I get a lot is about how the guys in the booth can tell what type of pitch was just thrown. It all starts before you set foot in the booth. First, you need to find out ahead of time what the pitcher's repertoire is. David Wells, for example, has a fastball and curve, but he also throws an occasional change-up, slider, or cutter. Now you know what your choices are. The next thing you have to do is hope for a good booth. When I was calling Yankees games, our booth was right behind home plate, which is how it is for most teams. That's ideal. Oftentimes when I'm working for MLB Network, we get the booth way off to the side, which makes this more difficult. Then you look at the catcher. You know a lot about what's coming just by where the catcher sets up. If a right-handed hitter is up and the catcher sets up on the inside part of the plate, that's not going to be a curveball. It's going to be a fastball. You don't throw your curveball to the inside part of the plate.

I also look for how the catcher's glove moves. That will ultimately determine the pitch. Let's say you have a left-handed pitcher (me), a right-handed hitter (Jeter), and a really smart catcher (Yogi Berra). Yogi sets up in middle of plate, and I throw my pitch. As it comes in, you see Yogi's glove move to the outside part of the plate. That's your clue that it is either a fastball that is moving away, or I just missed my target because a curveball would be breaking the other way—in toward Derek's hands. Of course, in that example, if I missed my spot, Derek has probably taken me to the opposite field for a base hit. But those are the things I use in the broadcast booth to tell if it's a fastball, a curve/slider, or a change-up.

Don't "Talk Back"

Just like the teams on the field, the production team will have its hits, runs, and errors during the course of the season. Most of the audience never even realizes that. But sometimes funny things happen that are too big to ignore. And the longer you work in the booth, the more the stories accumulate. Phil Rizzuto called Yankees games for more than 40 years, a fact that would probably elicit his famous "Holy cow." Because of his longevity, there are plenty of stories of funny things happening when "Scooter" was in the booth. Rizzuto was a heck of a ballplayer. A slick fielding shortstop and one of the all-time great bunters, he played his entire career from 1941–56 for the Yankees. And that was a good time to be a Yankee. He won seven World Series, including five straight from '49–'53. He's also another one of the Yankees from those dynasty years who earned AL MVP honors. Scooter got his in 1950. Legendary manager Casey Stengel had a chance to take Scooter after a tryout for the Brooklyn Dodgers in the '30s but didn't. After then managing him on the Yankees for years, Casey said of Rizzuto, "He is the greatest short-stop I have ever seen in my entire baseball career, and I have watched some beauties." Joe DiMaggio always said, "People loved watching me play baseball. Scooter, they just loved." The year after he retired, he was calling Yankees games along with Mel Allen and Red Barber. He would call games on TV and radio all the way until 1996, two years after his induction into Cooperstown.

How's This for a Record? Scooter never won a Gold Glove during his playing days, but he did earn a Gold Record. On Meat Loaf's *Bat Out of Hell* album released in 1977, that is Rizzuto calling the "action" in the double entendre-filled mock radio call on the song "Paradise By the Dashboard Light."

I got to work with Scooter and Bill White when I was hired by WPIX in 1986. The basic setup was a two-man booth; one would do play-by-play and describe the action, and the other would be the color analyst who would add insights in and around the action. And then the three of us would rotate. So if Bill and I did the first three innings, Bill and Scooter would do the next three, and Scooter and I would do the final three innings. And our rotation would change every game, but that was how we worked it.

Early that season the Yankees were playing the Indians, so we were in old Municipal Stadium in Cleveland. And the weather was bitter cold. The stadium held up to 70,000 for baseball; I think there were maybe 10,000 there. It felt empty. Scooter and I had the last three innings, and we were freezing in our booth. For me it was no big deal. This was a big job I landed, working for the Yankees, and I was still pretty excited to be there. Rizzuto had been doing this for decades at this point, so the excitement that was keeping me warm had worn off on him probably during the Nixon Administration. After the first half of the seventh inning, Scooter, who always referred to everyone by their last name, said to me, "Hey, Kaat, I'm going to the men's room. Cover for me." And off he went. Now I was a little concerned for two reasons. The first was I had never done play-by-play before. I had always done color. So I wasn't sure if I was the best guy to "cover" for Scooter. The other worry was I had heard stories of Scooter leaving games early. We were about to come back from commercial, and our producer Don Carney asked me over the headset, "Where's Rizzuto?" I said, "He went to the bathroom." I heard Don sigh and I knew in that moment that Rizzuto wasn't in the bathroom. He had gone outside, grabbed a cab, and went back to the hotel because it was too darn cold. I ended up doing the last three innings of the game by myself.

If you watch a broadcast carefully, you will notice that all announcers either have a headset on or an earpiece in their ear. This allows the director and producer and anyone else down in the TV truck to be able to talk to the announcers. Here in the U.S., sports announcers are often referred to by people in TV production as "the talent." I always thought that term was an odd choice. Yes, announcers need a certain amount of talent to do their job, but so does the director, the producer, or the stats guy or gal. They all have talent, so why aren't they called by that name? In the United Kingdom and Australia, they would call what I do being a "presenter." That seems to be a much more accurate and a less potentially offensive term, but it never caught on here. Thus, we will stick with this awkward American convention.

So the "talent" have their earpieces, which are called IFBs. It stands for "Interruptible Fold Back." One of the things you have to master if you are going to be on TV is being able to talk to the audience while someone else is talking in your ear through the IFB. I can tell you from experience, folks, it is not easy. When you hear Al Michaels, Brent Musburger, Joe Buck, or any of those big time play-by-play guys on the air, half of the time a producer is in their ear telling them what's coming up next. For any of you out there who want to be play-by-play announcers, practice talking to one buddy in front of you while another is talking to you on the phone in your ear. Master that and you are halfway home because it gets even more complicated. The producer can talk to all the talent at once or just one at a time. So even if you hear something in your ear, your partner may not.

If the talent has to talk to the producer for some reason while they are on the air, there is a "talk back" button. If you press this, it kills your individual microphone to the broadcast, but the producer can still hear you. Let's say Scooter was calling the action, and I wanted the producer to get a shot of the bullpen. While Scooter's said to you at home, "And here's the pitch…strike one," I'm on the talk back to the producer saying, "Mariano's warming up early—get a shot of it." The director finds a good shot on his wall of monitors, calls out "take Camera Two," and the TD switches it as I'm saying, "Scooter, I think Joe Torre's thinking about a change because Rivera's warming up out in the bullpen." But you have to press that button, or else Ma and Pa in Poughkeepsie are going to hear what you are saying to the truck. And there are things said that you definitely don't want Ma and Pa to hear.

For as long as Rizzuto was on television, he never really mastered the IFB and the talk back. But his charming manner usually got him out of a jam. A few years after I left WPIX, Tom Seaver joined Scooter and Bill in the three-man rotation in the booth. By this point Phil would usually get the first six innings and be allowed to leave by the seventh. In fact, they would often show a shot of the traffic on the George Washington Bridge from the top of Yankee Stadium in the later innings and say, "There goes Scooter now." But one time Scooter had the last six innings. And he was just finishing up the middle innings with Seaver, and Bill White was going to join him for the last three innings. Bill was an old pro and, unlike me back in Cleveland, he could handle

Legendary announcer Phil Rizzuto, with whom I had the pleasure of working when WPIX hired me in 1986, calls a game from the booth.

doing both play-by-play and color by himself. The Yankees were down 10–1, and Scooter was not looking forward to doing those last three innings in a blowout. So before Bill went up to the booth, he told the director John Moore that he'd do the last three innings solo so Scooter could leave early. Scooter was on the air with Seaver at the moment, and Seaver was telling a story when Moore told Scooter in his IFB, "Hey Scooter, you can take off at the end of the inning." Moore, being the good director, only said that into Rizzuto's earpiece—not Seaver's. Well Scooter was so excited to hear that he was going home early that he could've kissed Moore. So he does the next best thing and said, "Oh, I love you" over the air. Unfortunately, Scooter didn't hit the talk back. So for the viewer at home, they heard Seaver telling a story about the next batter, when all of sudden, Scooter blurted out, "Oh, I love you!" But Ma and Pa in Poughkeepsie weren't the only ones who were confused. Remember, Seaver didn't hear what John Moore said either.

He had no idea why Scooter was shouting these affections on the air. But Tom is a professional and responded, "Oh, Scooter...I'm fond of you, too." Rizzuto tried to explain himself to Seaver by saying, "I was talking to Moore." To which Seaver replied, "I'm sure he loves you, too." Something like that has happened to every announcer who has ever stepped in the booth.

Mastering the talk back is crucial to being an on-air personality. Another use for the talk back is to correct mistakes while you are on the air. If I hear my partner give an incorrect fact on the air, I quickly hit the talk back and tell the truck, "It was Smith, not Jones," and they immediately tell my partner in their ear to give him or her a chance to correct it. I, of course, expect the same courtesy. It is never good form to correct your partner on the air.

How many times have you heard an announcer cough or sneeze on the air? Not too often, if at all. That's because next to the talk back button there is a "cough" button. This kills your microphone to everyone—even the truck (they don't need to hear you sneeze either) so you can do what you have to do without blowing out anybody's ear or letting the home audience know your hay fever is coming on. The other time you use the cough button is if you get a case of the giggles. Let's face it. Sometimes something strikes you as funny, and you start laughing uncontrollably. It used to happen to me once in a while in church as a kid. Well, if it happens when you are on the air, you just hit the cough button until it passes and then get back to work.

Fair or Foul

As I said, the production side of things is a team as much as the ones on the field, and everyone has to do their part to get the right result. And just like a baseball team, all those pieces don't always get along 100 percent of the time. There are disagreements that have to be worked through just like any other team. When I was working for the YES Network, we would do a sponsored element called "Player of the Game" at the end of each broadcast. As the game got into the later innings, the producer, Kevin Smollon, or the director, Bill Webb, would hit me on the talk back and ask, "Kitty, who is your Player of the Game?" Well, during this one particular game, I said, "No doubt, it's pitcher Tanyon Sturtze. He had three innings of shutout ball. He is my Player of the Game." So the guys in the truck start building a package of clips for the end of the game as we always did. Then in the bottom of the eighth inning and with the Yankees up by three runs, Gary Sheffield hit a home run to make it a four-run lead, which did not really impact the game. Then Leon says to me, "I just got a call from John Filippelli." I knew right away I wasn't going to like that. John was our executive producer or EP. So if the producer is the manager, then the EP is the GM. He's my boss's boss. And like a GM, the EP is the one who takes a broad view of the production team and the entire season and usually does not get involved in the day-to-day producing of the show. That's why he has the producer/manager. Filippelli was not that kind of EP. He would often stand in the booth between announcers and try to put words in our mouths. It would be like Brian Cashman sitting in the dugout telling pitchers what to throw. It never made any sense to me. What he thought was the proper thing to do on the air, and what I thought didn't always jibe, and eventually our two ways of doing things would clash.

Kevin said Filippelli wanted to change the Player of the Game to Sheffield because of the home run. John knew that Steinbrenner liked Sheffield and thought it would please George to see Gary as the Player of the Game. I said, "Kevin, you are in tough position because you have to do what Filippelli says, but I can't in good conscience say Shef is the Player of the Game. It wouldn't be accurate." I didn't want to get Kevin in trouble, so I said, "You guys build the package for Sheffield, and I'll figure out how to handle it."

The game ends, and Michael Kay said, "Here's Jim with the Player of the Game." I get on the microphone and say, "There's been a change. Someone stuffed the ballet box, and for some reason Gary Sheffield has been named Player of the Game for his solo shot in bottom of the eighth. But any of you who, watched this game and know baseball, know the real Player of the Game was Tanyon Sturtze for his three shutout innings." I had come to that fine line as a broadcaster between defying authority and not letting someone ruin your credibility by putting words in your mouth that you know are not accurate. Because, as a broadcaster, at the end of the day, your credibility is all that you have. I don't want people at home saying, "How in the world can he name Sheffield as Player of the Game when Sturtze was the one who turned it around?" So if the Yankees of the '70s could have Billy and Reggie butting heads, I guess the YES Network of the 2000s could have me and Filippelli.

I don't want you to give the impression that just because there's a microphone in front of me that I can say whatever I want. A loose cannon on the air doesn't really help anybody. Words have repercussions. And I freely admit that I have stepped over a line a time or two—but never intentionally. While I was working for the MSG Network and we were still doing games out of the old Yankee Stadium, there was a lot of talk of building a new stadium downtown. And Steinbrenner was actively lobbying to secure city funds to help him do it. At the same time, the city of Charlotte had just shot down using public taxpayer funds to build a new stadium to try and attract the Minnesota Twins to move to Charlotte. My comment about this on the air, which was an indirect message to Steinbrenner, was "Well, the people of Charlotte have spoken, and it's probably true all over the county. Mr. Owner, if you want a brand new stadium, spend your own money and don't ask us for our taxpayer money."

What I didn't know at the time was MSG was going through some negotiations with George over rights to air Yankees games in the future.

I ended up getting a call from Mike McCarthy, who was our executive producer at MSG. He said, "Jim, I never want to tell you what to say or not to say. But let me ask you favor. If the issue comes up again, can you try not to make too big a topic of it because Steinbrenner is sensitive on the subject of trying to get taxpayer money, and we are trying to negotiate a contract to extend our rights to Yankees games? So it behooves us to keep a nice, smooth relationship with him." And I had no problem with that. I definitely didn't want to rock the boat as I loved my time at MSG. And the topic wasn't critical to what we were doing so we dropped it. But the incident highlights the impact you can have on things you aren't even trying to affect when you speak into a microphone for a living.

A Perfect Broadcast

I've called a few perfect games in my time—as rare as those are. But I'm not talking about those here. I'm talking about a "perfect broadcast." Since the game is unscripted, it's difficult to have a hard and fast plan going in other than "follow the ball." Through the years, though, this is the template that I found works the best.

Opening

I try to give fans a reason to watch the upcoming game—like an intense rivalry, a great pitching matchup, etc. I may offer a comment or two on what players to watch that night because they have really been productive lately.

First Three Innings

These are usually full of housekeeping items like the lineups, commentary on a few characteristics of the pitchers, profiles of the managers, and strengths and weaknesses of each team. I'd also have the keys for each team to win that night's game.

Middle Innings

I rely on the score to give me direction. If it's a close game, I focus on the managers' strategy or the pitching strategy vs. key hitters. This is where you can really get inside baseball kind of stuff for the fans.

Final Three Innings

If it's a close game, I want to talk about who is in the bullpen for each team, the potential hitters on the bench, the thinking of the managers. It's also a good idea to recap what has happened since the first inning for those who tuned in late. As the game comes to an end, I want to "pay off" what I said in the first part of the game about keys for each team and how those came to fruition. Did the pitcher-hitter matchups affect the outcome as I thought?

At the very end, I let the producer and director show crowd and dugout reaction pictures and players in the field shots to give the audience a glimpse of winners and losers and to get the emotions on screen. While closing games out, I always reflected on my friend Ray Scott's minimalistic style and tried my best to let the pictures tell the story.

In a blowout game, the above template goes in the trash bin, and the announcers can begin to tell stories—any stories—that may keep the audience interested, even though the game on the field is no longer compelling. That's where all my years in baseball definitely come in handy.

An Analyst's Analysis

People will sometimes ask me, "Hey Kitty, why don't you have a signature call?" The answer is very simple: I never wanted one. To me the game is always about the players and their teams, not the announcers. I always wanted more emphasis put on the ball than on me. Don't get me wrong. Voices like the great Vin Scully can definitely help make the experience more enjoyable. But whether or not someone says, "Back,

back, back" or "Good-bye, Mr. Spalding" doesn't change the fact that people are really tuning in to see if their team wins the game or not—end of story. I've even worked with directors who would say, "Kitty, what are we going to do today to put our stamp on the broadcast? What are we looking for?" And I'd say, "I'm looking for the first pitch of the game and then I'm going to follow the ball wherever it goes." In tennis, basketball, and football, it just goes side to side and usually in an intended direction. In baseball it goes all over the place. Even the batter doesn't know where it's going to go most of the time. Trying to put a stamp on something so unpredictable feels forced to me. The ball is the star, not us. In my book, less is more for a good telecast.

I've been involved in professional baseball as a player, coach, and broadcaster for 57 years and I know things are going to change in more than a half century. But there is a trend I see in broadcasting these days that makes me worried. When I became a professional ballplayer, I spent parts of four seasons in the minors. That's where I really started learning how to pitch. And once I got to the big leagues, I kept on learning. I would get as close to the greats and learn as much as I could from them, always asking questions. The same was true when I became an announcer. I didn't start on a nationally televised Game of the Week. I started doing the College World Series on ESPN back in the mid-1980s (when people were still trying figure out what ESPN stood for). I just sat in the truck and listened and watched producer Fred Gaudelli and director Marc Payton work several games. That's how and where I learned to use the talk back button. I also saw how things get hectic and fast and furious in the production truck, even though the game may be progressing at a snail's pace. When I first began to do games on a regular basis, it was gratifying to hear producers say, "Kitty, you use the talk back key real well." I'd say, "Thanks, I learned how from Fred Gaudelli." Fred went on to become the producer for *Monday Night Football* on ABC before moving over to *Sunday Night Football* on NBC and has been there ever since. He is one of the best at incorporating all of the newest technology but keeping the old school feel of the telecast. Chris Pfeiffer at MLB Network keeps that same follow-the-ball feel to the games he does.

I continued to learn the mechanics and the timing necessary from watching, listening, and working with legendary announcers like Dick Enberg, Dick Stockton, and John Madden. I learned so much from players-turned-analysts like Tony Kubek and Tim McCarver. And I'd pick the brain of award-winning producers such as Harry Coyle, Joe Aceti, Gene Kirby, and Fred Gaudelli. From these great men, I learned there are fundamentals for covering a game just as there are for playing it:

- Get in and out in eight seconds.
- Don't talk over pitches.
- Don't start a story with two outs.
- Don't analyze the play that just happened until the director gets to show reactions from the players, the fans, the dugouts, and whatever else that's interesting.

The technology available now—the high-speed cameras, high-definition picture, the tools that producers and directors have at their disposal—makes the games more entertaining and compelling to watch. However, I find that many of the younger generation of announcers haven't been trained the same way. As a result the game has become more talk television and less follow the ball. I have worked with guys who consistently talk over pitches or bring an agenda into the booth, coming in with copious notes. Sometimes it feels like they are trying to impress the audience with their knowledge instead of following the game.

The main difference between the new generation of player-turned-announcers and the older set can be summed up in a single word: curiosity. The great pitching coach Eddie Lopat told me in the early '60s, "Kid, if you don't have any arm problems, you're going to pitch in the big leagues a long time." When I asked him why, he said, "Because you are curious about how to get better." That was me alright. Put me anywhere near great pitchers like Spahn, Roberts, Ford, or even my peers like Dave McNally, and I was watching and asking questions. It was the same with my broadcasting career. Enberg taught me about not jumping in too soon after a play to analyze it. Not keeping a lot of notes—I learned that when I called John Madden to pick his brain. He was kind enough to spend a lot of time on the phone with me and convince me that if I did my homework and was prepared in all areas of the upcoming game I wouldn't need notes. He'd say, "If you write it down, you'll try to force it in. If you forgot it, it probably wasn't that important."

The late, great Gene Kirby, who used to work with Dizzy Dean, always liked to call out play-by-play announcers when they would use a bad cliché like, "That's down the line, into the corner, and that's trouble." Gene would reply, "Trouble for who? The guy that hit it doesn't think it was trouble." That might sound like nitpicking, but it does point out when doing play-by-play, less is more. Just follow the ball and react accordingly. When I do play-by-play, that's what I try to do. And pretty soon you get into a nice rhythm. That's why it's important for the color man to not talk over pitches. It breaks up the tempo. I've worked with some big name color commentators who consistently talk over pitches and are not really paying attention to the play on the field. That makes it really tough to keep the flow of the game.

You have to let the telecast breathe. I think that's so much nicer than having the producer yell in your ear, "Shut the f--- up!" And never talk down to the viewer. If there is a cardinal sin in the booth, that is it. Another thing that would help a young broadcaster would be to go sit in the production truck for a few games. Seeing and becoming familiar with that side of things will only help you in the booth. And even though you may want to, don't let your first game be a Game 7 of the World Series. Cut your teeth in the minors, and your fans will thank you throughout your career. And most of all...be curious. When the Yankees network began to bring in former players like John Flaherty, Joe Girardi, David Cone, Paul O'Neill, and Al Leiter, they would ask me for a little direction regarding the fundamentals of broadcasting. It's interesting when you look at that list of players. To steal a line from the great Scully, they were all players who took pride in getting better.

My approach to each game I announced was to imagine I was sitting in box seats with three fans. One was at their very first baseball game, another was an average fan, the last was a true baseball junkie. Before the game was over, my goal was to give each one of those three fans something about the game they might not know. The real reward is when I am stopped on the street by a fan who tells me, "Thanks for not talking down to me. You just talk like you're sitting next to me." Guess what, kid...I am.

CHAPTER 8
COMPANY MEN

If you can keep your head when all about you
Are losing theirs and blaming it on you,
If you can trust yourself when all men doubt you,
But make allowance for their doubting too;
If you can wait and not be tired by waiting,
Or being lied about, don't deal in lies,
Or being hated, don't give way to hating,

—*Rudyard Kipling*

That's how Rudyard Kipling begins his brilliant poem *If.* Published in 1910 it was written as a father's advice to a son. But if you look at the words closely, it could also be used as a job description for working with the New York Yankees during the reign of George Steinbrenner, one of the most complicated men in the history of sports. He was an imperfect leader who pushed incessantly for perfection in others; a no-nonsense, hands-on owner who achieved his greatest success when his hands were tied; and impatient to a fault but also generous beyond belief. As a player and broadcaster, I have seen all sides of George, and my opinion of him has gone from one extreme to the other and back...and back again. To put it simply, with George there were only two ways to go: you either made history or you *were* history.

George grew up in Cleveland, a die-hard Indians fan. But that didn't stop him as a kid from running to the Cleveland Hotel every time the Yankees came to town to try to catch a glimpse of those legendary Bronx Bombers walking through the lobby. Even at a young age, he knew there was something different about those guys in pinstripes. He learned his hard-nosed leadership style from one of the hardest there was. When he was at Ohio State, Steinbrenner served as a graduate assistant under legendary football coach Woody Hayes. The Buckeyes went undefeated that year, winning the Rose Bowl and were declared national champions. So George saw what could be accomplished with a take-no-prisoners attitude. Steinbrenner made his fortune in shipping and shipbuilding and in 1973 he used the wealth he had made to lead a group that bought the Yankees from CBS for $10 million. *Forbes Magazine* now estimates the team's worth at more than $1.5 billion. His 37 years at the helm were the longest in Yankees history. From the start George always thought it wasn't enough to just be a ballclub in New York. You had to have flare. You had to put on a show. He was competing with Broadway and 30 Rock as much as he was Boston and Baltimore. His franchise had a tradition of winning, and he knew the power that it had over people and the feeling of awe it inspired. (He had felt it himself at the Cleveland Hotel.) Now it was his job to bring that feeling back. As George had said, "Owning the Yankees is like owning the Mona Lisa." His journey to return the team to its glory days would have more ups and downs than a yo-yo convention, and along the way, it would change the game itself.

Impatience Is a Virtue

There's that old saying about San Francisco in the summer time: if you don't like the weather, wait five minutes. The same could almost be said about Yankees managers in the first few decades of George's tenure with the Yankees. From 1973 through 1996, Steinbrenner changed managers a remarkable 20 times. He hired and fired Billy Martin alone five times. I had firsthand experience of George's impatience with Yankees skippers. I played with the Yankees from May of '79 to April of '80 and I had three different managers in less than a season. To put it in perspective, I've included a timeline of George's rule in the Bronx later in this chapter. You can see he should have replaced the door to the manager's office with a turnstile.

Another area where George's impatience really showed was in developing talent. He had a hard time waiting for a young player to turn into a great professional—when there were already great and proven talents out there already. Of course, those talents played for other teams, and trading for them was complicated. If you didn't have the pieces in your franchise that the other team needed, then that player you were salivating over would be going somewhere else.

When I signed my first major league contract, it contained the infamous reserve clause. This meant that even at the end of the term of my contract, the ballclub retained my rights. I couldn't talk to another team, and no other team could talk to me. This clause could trace its roots all the way back to the 1870s, and it protected clubs at the expense of players. There was no incentive for teams to pay their players more than they wanted. No one else could make them a better offer. The player's only option was to hold out—or refuse to play. But then you are not making any money, so even that wasn't much of an option. The St. Louis Cardinals' Curt Flood had sued commissioner Bowie Kuhn to try and change that, saying the reserve clause violated his rights. The case went all the way to the Supreme Court in 1972. But the court decided in baseball's favor. Although it helped bring national attention to the issue, it would be a few more years before the dreaded reserve clause was removed.

It was the end of the 1974 season, and the Oakland A's had just won their third straight title on the back of its Cy Young winning pitcher Jim "Catfish" Hunter. But Catfish wasn't feeling too appreciated because half of his $100,000 salary, which was supposed to go toward paying a life insurance annuity, hadn't been paid by the team. After repeated requests by Hunter, all A's owner Charlie Finley would say was, "The check was in the mail." But it wasn't. That's when the executive director of the players' association—the great Marvin Miller—saw an opportunity. By not paying Catfish on time, the notoriously cheap Finley was in violation of the contract he signed with Jim. And the penalty for that violation was

Like many players, I had my ups and downs with George Steinbrenner, who reigned over the Yankees for more than 30 years.

also in the contract. It said that Catfish would become a free agent. An arbiter agreed, and the best pitcher in baseball was suddenly on the market. As Hunter said to his wife after he got the news, "We don't belong to anybody." George would make sure that feeling wouldn't last for long.

Because of the reserve clause, very few players had agents back then. So as the first superstar free agent in baseball history, Jim hired tobacco and peanut lawyer J. Carlton Cherry, who lived near Jim's North Carolina home, to hear offers for his services. San Diego Padres owner Ray Kroc and his McDonald's money came calling first and offered him a $4 million deal. Then in walked Clyde Klutz. Clyde was a former catcher and longtime scout. He was the man who signed Hunter to his very first contract and he was sent to that small country lawyer's office by none other than Steinbrenner. It was a brilliant move by George, using both money and sentiment to outfox his fellow owner. After a few conversations with Clyde, Jim wanted nothing to do with San Diego and everything to do with the Yankees. On New Year's Eve, the Yankees announced their $3.75 million acquisition. And baseball has never been the same since. Every free agent owes a debt to Miller, Catfish, and Steinbrenner.

There were other times where George's inability to sit still ended up helping the team like during the players' strike in 1981. When the players walked out for 50 days, all of the Yankees coaches and managers were still getting paid. George never liked to pay people to do nothing, so he sent his entire coaching staff down to the minors, assigning them to teams in the Yankees farm system to help evaluate talent. Yogi Berra was sent to the Double A Nashville Sounds in the Southern League. At the time future Yankees manager Stump Merrill was in charge. A catcher by trade, though he never got out of the minors, Merrill could not believe that a Yankees legend—No. 8 himself—had come into his office and asked, "What can I do for you?" One of the things Yogi did was to evaluate a young first baseman that the Yankees brass weren't very high on. Berra thought the kid was quite good with both the glove and the bat.

He said he'd make a great major leaguer and that the club should hang on to him. That "kid" was Don Mattingly. And that's why Mattingly wears No. 8 as manager of the Los Angeles Dodgers.

George and Yogi had a rocky relationship, and much of it was due to how Steinbrenner handled firing Berra in 1985. Yogi had had a rough time as manager in '84. He was constantly being compared to Martin and his successes, and yet Yogi had nowhere near the roster that Billy had. Still George assured the Yankees icon that he would be hands-off in '85 and let Yogi finish the season. Of course, promises to managers from George are a lot like playing the shell games you see along Times Square. The promise is right there in front of you. You see it with your own two eyes, but after a few things move around, you lift that shell, and there's nothing there.

Sixteen games into the '85 season, the Yankees sat at 6–10 after a sweep by the White Sox in Chicago, and Steinbrenner fired Yogi and replaced him with Martin (Billy's fourth stint at the helm if you are scoring at home). Yogi understood that's the nature of being a manager, especially in the Bronx. He'd been fired as Yankees manager in 1964—back when George was still building ships in Cleveland. But Yogi had won more World Series with the Yankees than anyone else in history. You had to think he deserved a call from Steinbrenner himself. In direct contrast, when the New York Mets were about to fire Berra in '75, Mets owner Donald Grant learned from Yogi's wife, Carmen, that her parents were about to come for a visit and that it would be tough on Yogi to be let go with the in-laws in town. Grant called back a few weeks later to see if it was a better time. Would the Boss be that thoughtful? Not this time. George didn't even make the call. He had general manager Clyde King tell Yogi he was out. It was a terrible slight by Steinbrenner, and it led to a 14-year rift between Yogi and George.

You want to talk about Yankees pride? Yogi had plenty of it and he would not relent. When they put his plaque in Monument Park along with his mentor Bill Dickey, Yogi didn't come. When his best friend

Phil Rizzuto had his 50th wedding anniversary at the stadium, Yogi didn't come. When they started winning World Series and Joe Torre asked Yogi to come by and talk to the guys, Yogi didn't come. Except for the funerals of Billy Martin and Mickey Mantle, Yogi didn't lay eyes on George for almost a decade and a half. For many of those who had to deal with George up close and in person, Yogi's "holdout" was a point of pride. As Mattingly put it, "It is a deep and profound joy that Yogi won't sell out." It wasn't until January of '99 that the feud finally came to an end. But it took George flying to New Jersey to apologize to Yogi face to face. And that was the other side of George. He could make a brilliant mistake, but he could also admit it and fix it.

Steinbrenner's dealings sometimes involved funny stories, too. Lou Piniella was negotiating a contract with GM Gabe Paul, and the two sides were still a ways apart. Lou and Gabe met over Chinese food to try and work it out. As the meal was winding down, Gabe offered to split the difference between their two numbers. As he cracked open his fortune cookie, Lou still wasn't sure. Then he unrolled and read his fortune, which said, "Be happy with what you have." Sweet Lou took that as a sign and accepted the Yankees' offer.

George also had a sense for the dramatic. When he signed a big free agent, he scheduled the press conference—down to the minute—to ensure maximum positive effect in the New York press. The same was true when he wanted to bury a story. Like in 2001 after Derek Jeter took the Boss for a cool $189 million, Steinbrenner announced the deal during a press conference late on a Friday afternoon after most people were dashing off to start their weekend, and only the skinny Saturday edition of the papers—the ones with the smallest circulation—would have it in print. As Jeter's agent Casey Close said, "If you can sweep a $189 million contract under the rug, that's when you would do it."

Of course, sometimes his use of the press could backfire. When the Yankees lost to the Dodgers in the 1981 World Series, Steinbrenner publicly apologized for his team's performance in the papers. Players, press, and fans alike lined up to criticize him for that one.

Unfamiliar Rings   As owner of the Yankees, George Steinbrenner won seven World Series. But did you know he has won titles on the ice and the hardwood as well? Steinbrenner was part of a membership group that owned the New Jersey Devils when they won the Stanley Cup in 2003. And the first professional franchise George owned was the Cleveland Pipers of the American Basketball League. With future NBA Hall of Famer Jerry Lucas leading the way, the Pipers won the 1962 ABL crown. Unfortunately, there wasn't much time to celebrate the victory. By the end of the year, the league had folded.

Another thing about George I'll never forget was his rules. George had plenty of them, including his infamous grooming policy. If you were going to work for the Yankees as a player, coach, or executive, you were forbidden to have facial hair other than a moustache, and the hair on your head better not reach your collar, or you'd get a phone call. This rule started the day George showed up in New York. The story goes that on Opening Day in '73, when players removed their caps for the national anthem, George saw several players breaking his grooming code. But back then he didn't know the players yet and without names on the jerseys he could only write down their numbers. Not long after that, Ralph Houk, the manager, got a note demanding numbers 1, 15, and 28 cut their hair immediately. (For the record that was Bobby Murcer, Thurman Munson, and Sparky Lyle, respectively.) What a way to spend Opening Day. In '83 Goose Gossage started growing a beard. Yogi, on Steinbrenner's orders, reminded Gossage that it could only be a mustache—no chin whiskers. So Goose shaved his chin and left the rest. That giant biker stache that remained is pretty much how most people picture Goose to this day. Gossage has George to thank for his distinctive look.

Even Donnie Baseball wasn't above the law when it came to hair below the collar. In '91 Mattingly was growing his hair in the fashion of the day, which just happened to be the (now unfashionable) mullet, which meant short in front and long in the back. At the time Steinbrenner was suspended from day-to-day operations, but he had a hair up his you-know-what about Mattingly's hair. Yankees management told Don to cut it; Mattingly refused and he was benched and fined $250. The New York media had a field day with this. Phil Rizzuto, along with his WPIX booth mates, Murcer and Tom Seaver, had fun with it before a game, and Scooter dressed up as a barber. It's hard to say who won this one. Mattingly returned—with his mullet intact—the next game and received a standing ovation from the fans. But a few days later, he trimmed it.

When Johnny Damon helped the Red Sox end the Curse of the Bambino in 2004, his appearance drew comparisons to a caveman and Jesus. But soon after he signed a four-year, $52 million contract with the Yankees in December of 2005, a clean-shaven and neatly trimmed Damon showed up at his press conference in the Bronx. As George said at the time, "He looks like a Yankee. He sounds like a Yankee. He is a Yankee." (In Boston the reaction was quite different. Red Sox fans displayed their disapproval of the defection of their gritty but notoriously weak-armed center fielder by wearing T-shirts with Damon's picture on it saying, "Looks like Jesus, Acts like Judas, Throws like Mary.") It makes you wonder what George would have done if he had all of those Boston players who won the World Series in 2013 sporting those *Duck Dynasty*-like beards. Would the sheer volume of shearing be too much for even the Boss? Would his love of championships or chins win out? I know Joe DiMaggio's nickname is safe, but you could make an argument to give Steinbrenner the title of "Yankee Clipper."

My first run-in with George had nothing to do with facial hair. It was at the end of the 1979 season. After back-to-back titles, the Yankees suffered the tragic loss of Thurman Munson and finished in fourth place, 13½ games behind the Baltimore Orioles. I had made it into 40 games that season for the Yankees—all but one in relief. That September I did what I always did when my contract was up: I went to the manager to see what his plans were for me the next season. I talked to Martin, who had returned to replace Bob Lemon halfway through the season. Billy said he wanted me back and to go talk to George. So I went to see "the Boss." I had exchanged pleasantries with Steinbrenner a few times by this point, but this was my first one-on-one meeting with him. I called him George. Not Boss or Mr. Steinbrenner. For some reason I always called my owners—whether it was Ruly Carpenter of the Philadelphia Phillies, Calvin Griffith of the Minnesota Twins, or John Allyn of the White Sox—by their first name.

George and I looked over the numbers. He offered me a 13 percent cost of living increase, taking my salary from $150,000 to $168,000. I thought that sounded fair. But there was a catch. George wanted to protect some young players from waivers, so he said, "I'm going to take you off the roster, but I'll put you back on in December after the waiver period ends." Again, that made sense. I thanked him and went off to enjoy the offseason. I don't remember exactly what I did, but I know I enjoyed the down time more than Martin, who ended up punching a marshmallow salesman named Joseph Cooper, leading George to fire him for the second time. Meanwhile, instead of getting a contract in the mail, I recieved a letter from new Yankees GM Gene Michael inviting me to spring training as a non-roster player. I called Michael, asking, "Didn't George tell you the deal we made back in September?" He hadn't heard a thing about it. When I called George down in Tampa, I found out why Michael hadn't heard. *George didn't remember it ever happening.* He was rather adamant that we never talked, and there was no way for me to convince him. So now I was in a tough spot. The re-entry draft had already happened. I had no choice but to show up for spring training without a contract and try and earn a spot. But I sure wasn't happy about it. Somewhere along the line, though, George must have remembered our talk because I got a $5,000 bonus check out of the blue. And George never paid a player a dime he didn't have to.

I ended up having a strong spring, pitching 20 or so scoreless innings. I didn't give them a chance to cut me. So Gene Michael finally hands me a contract…for the same amount I made last season. I told him George had promised $168,000. Gene goes back George and returns to me and says, "George says sign the contract or he is pulling the offer." And that was my first experience with George. Needless to say, it left a bad taste in my mouth. Before the first month of the season was over, I was shipped off to St. Louis. A few angry letters and phone calls to Steinbrenner after I left didn't fix anything, but they did make me feel a little better. I definitely thought that would be my last dealing with the Boss.

Boy, was I wrong.

I wasn't the only one who ran into George's "selective memory" around contract time. At the end of the 1980 season, Steinbrenner grabbed headlines by snagging yet another high-priced free agent. Dave Winfield would eventually end up in Cooperstown. But even if you knew that back then, you'd have thought $23 million for 10 years was a lot. And it was. Winfield was the highest paid player in the game. But five years into that contract, Winfield had not brought home any championships. And an impatient George decided to stir the pot a little. In a September article in *The New York Times*, Steinbrenner said: "Where is Reggie Jackson? We need a Mr. October or a Mr. September. Winfield is Mr. May."

Ouch. I have never owned a major league franchise, but I'm pretty sure you can't call out your top guy like that and expect a positive reaction. But then again, the two had already butted heads. Dave wrote in his book, *Winfield, a Player's Life*, that back in 1982, Steinbrenner flatly refused to pay a $300,000 contribution to the Winfield Foundation that the Yankees were contractually obligated to pay. Winfield made it his mission to get George to keep his end of the deal and eventually got a court order to have the Boss pay up. If you asked Steinbrenner what he hated more than anything in the world, he'd tell you it's to lose. George hired a gambler by the name of Howie Spira and paid him $40,000 to dig up dirt on Winfield. When Major League Baseball commissioner Fay Vincent found out, he had Steinbrenner permanently banned from the day-to-day operations of the team. He still owned the team, but on July 30th, 1990, George had to hand the keys to the Yankees over and let someone else drive. As for Winfield, the whole thing left such a bad taste in his mouth that when he was inducted into the Hall of Fame in 2001, he did so as a Padre—not a Yankee.

The ban was a hard to pill to swallow for George. He loved being in charge of this world famous organization. He always said, "There are ballplayers, and then there are Yankees." But the Yankees hadn't been the Yankees since 1981, and a lot of that had to do with George. If you look at the won/loss records from 1982–1995, New York was one of the worst teams in the American League. With his hands on the wheel, the franchise kept trading away talented young players for high-priced free agents, and those deals were not paying off in championships. By 1990 the Yankees farm system was pretty bare. But then Steinbrenner was banned, and before you knew it, the Yankees front office was practicing patience. With Gene Michael and other executives running the show, suddenly the team could develop young players in house. If George had kept day-to-day control of the team, I doubt that we would have ever seen Bernie Williams in pinstripes. Or perhaps even Derek Jeter. Vincent's ban was lifted in 1993—when George posed as Napoleon for a *Sports Illustrated* cover announcing his return—and even then he let Michael and company continue doing what they were doing. And what they were doing was building an organization designed for winning championships.

My second announcing career with the Yankees coincided with their championship runs, and this time around, I learned a valuable lesson about George. It was April of 2002, and the Yankees were playing the Orioles in the Bronx. Rick Bauer was the pitcher of record for Baltimore when he left the game with a lead in the seventh inning. Bauer had pitched a few times at the end of the previous season and tallied five losses and a no decision. He was still looking for his first win in the majors. I got my first win at Yankee Stadium, so I knew exactly what he was going through. I told the producer to get some shots of Bauer on the bench as he watched the last few innings. He was chewing on his fingers, running his hands through his hair—all those nervous gestures that I probably did 42 years before as I sat on the verge of my first big league victory coming at Yankee Stadium. I pointed this out to the audience, helping them get an inside look into the game.

Then one of Steinbrenner's executives tells the production team, "George is down in Tampa and he wonders if this is an Orioles telecast." The message was clear. George thought I was paying too much attention to the Orioles' side of the story instead of the Yankees'. I didn't think that was the case at all, so between innings I asked this executive for Steinbrenner's cell phone number. I had no problem calling him directly and explaining what I was doing. The front office guys said, "Don't worry, we'll handle it." A week later, I was riding down the elevator at the stadium. George got on, and I saw my opportunity. "So George," I said, "I understand you were upset about something I said last week on the Orioles telecast."

George looked at me and said, "Jimmy, I'm never upset with what you say. You tell it like it is. I wish more people did." It was quite a revelation. I knew that George liked to keep people on edge. He thought if you were always in fear for your job you would do your best work. But this experience taught me that the executives were so concerned with what George *might* think and that he *might* call that they'd pre-empt it and say George wasn't happy with something when in fact he hadn't called.

The fear of George could be felt by almost anyone involved with the Yankees. It could even be found all the way up in the broadcast booth. During those glory years in the late '90s, we'd have a shot almost every game of Joe Torre and Don Zimmer in the dugout talking. In reality, they could be talking about anything from pitching to horseracing; we didn't have a mic on them. Don certainly knew his stuff and made a lot of suggestions to Joe, and Joe often followed them. During a mini-slump, questions about Joe's job security began to circulate in the press because Lord knows George wanted to win every year. This time Zimmer exploded. "I'm getting tired of this," he said. "Why is it when we win it's the geniuses down in Tampa who get the credit and when we lose it's always Joe Torre's fault?"

At the time we were in Cincinnati getting ready for an inter-league game when I got a call from our executive producer on the YES Network, John Filippelli. He said Steinbrenner was very upset with what Don had said, so we were not going to show that stock shot of Torre and Zimmer in Cincinnati because he didn't want that to spark a discussion. We were to keep Zimmer off our air. I said, "John, this is going to be a problem. Zim was born and raised in Cincinnati. Torre has already decided that Zimmer would bring out the lineup card. This is going to be a high moment for Zimmer, coming in with the Yankees to the town he grew up in. I cannot in good conscience do three Yankees games here in Cincy and *not* mention Don Zimmer." Filippelli said those were the orders, and that's what we were going to do.

I gave it some thought and came to the conclusion that I just couldn't risk my credibility as a broadcaster to let something so obvious go unsaid just because it might upset George. So I called Leon Hendry, who was the head of the YES Network, and I asked for a three-day leave of absence.

I told him I could not be forced to not mention Zimmer during those games. Leon gave me his full support. "Do the games, Jim. Say whatever you want to say. If there is any blowback from Steinbrenner, I'll handle it." In the end Zim took out the card, we covered it, and nothing was heard from the Boss' camp. It did, however, create a rift between me and Fillipelli because I went over his head to his boss. But I felt I had no choice. Unless I was breaking the law, I didn't like someone telling me what I could or could not say on the air. Bill White had always told me, "Don't let people put words in your mouth." This time I learned not to let them take them out either. But it all arose because of a fear of upsetting George.

As serious as George was, he could also poke fun at himself. There were those famous commercials with Billy Martin where they came down on opposite sides of the Miller Lite "Tastes Great/Less Filling" debate. With both sharing a tiny table at a bar, George and Billy were all smiles and laughing when they say they agree on "just about everything," including the beer they drink. But Billy said the best thing about the beer is it's "less filling" while George said it "tastes great." The smiles were replaced with shouts until George said, "Billy...you're fired." Billy's response: "Not again."

And then there was the whole *Seinfeld* thing. The critically acclaimed NBC sitcom was a fan favorite and a huge success through most of the '90s. In season five Jerry's best friend, George Costanza, gets a job as the assistant traveling secretary for the Yankees. Over the next few years and with the use of a body double and a voice-over impersonation, *Seinfeld* turned Steinbrenner into a Pat Benatar-singing, Communist-fearing, calzone-loving executive who even called Babe Ruth "nothing more than a fat old man with little girl legs." According to sportscaster Suzyn Waldman, the only thing Steinbrenner didn't like about his portrayal on *Seinfeld* was the sound of his voice. But the Boss couldn't do much about it because he was portrayed by *Seinfeld* boss and co-creator Larry David.

After several seasons the real Steinbrenner agreed to do a cameo on the show and even shot a few scenes with Elaine where he offered to take her to Costanza's wedding. He brilliantly lampooned himself, but in typical Steinbrenner fashion, he didn't like some of the plot twists the writers put in the episode and requested that his scenes not be used. But the parody continued all the way until the final episode of the legendary show.

George continued to be the man behind the Yankees throughout their recent glory years. He also continued his habit of quietly helping others. Sure, there were press releases of the Yankees donating to any number of charities. But whispers around the franchise over the years also noted that he paid the hospital bills for an employee or made contributions to the foundation fighting the disease that took the child of someone in the organization. That's the side of George that doesn't always see the light of day, but it is just as much a part of the man as all the firings.

As George started having health problems, he spent less and less time around the Yankees. In 2008 he handed control of the team over to his youngest son, Hal. I had retired from the YES Network in 2006 so I never got to know Hal or his older brother, Hank, who also worked for the club. My closest relationship in his family—and that was just through meeting him and visiting occasionally—was Steve Swindal, George's son-in-law. Steve married Jennifer Steinbrenner and, like George, he used to work with boats. Steve ran a marine towing company in Tampa. George named him a general partner from 1998 to 2006 and then made him chairman of the team's holding company, Yankee Global Enterprises, LLC. In 2005 George officially named Steve his successor. But marital trouble between Steve and Jennifer arose. When Swindal was busted for DUI in February of 2007, it wasn't long before he was pushed out. Hal Steinbrenner became more active in the team after Steve's arrest, but I was gone before all of that.

In 2009 Hal oversaw the Yankees move into their new stadium. He would end the season raising the World Series trophy, the 27th in

Yankees history. Hal wasted no time in dedicating the win to his father. It was as fitting a tribute as there ever was. On July 13th, 2010, the day of baseball's All-Star Game, the most famous owner in professional sports, George Michael Steinbrenner III, passed away near his home in Tampa, Florida. He was 80 years old. It was without a doubt an end of an era—not just for the Yankees, but for baseball as a whole.

Over the years my relationship with George went from rocky and distrustful to one of mutual respect. When I retired as a Yankees broadcaster in 2006, he went out of his way to ensure I had a fitting send-off. If he knew you were strong in your convictions, weren't intimidated, and told it like it was, he respected you. It really takes a few years in pinstripes to be able to sum up Steinbrenner. Upon George's death, Gossage said, "George *was* the Yankees. You loved and hated him at the same time." Ron "Gator" Guidry, who worked for George as a player, coach, and instructor for more than 35 years, said fittingly, "No matter what he appeared on the outside, he was good on the inside." But perhaps the best line came—as they often do—from Yogi. The beloved Yankee with 10 rings and a 14-year period of bad blood with George said upon his passing, "I wish I could have played for him."

Managing Chaos

John McMullen has a famous quote about Steinbrenner. Before owning the Houston Astros, McMullen was a minority owner with the Yankees when he said, "There is nothing more limited than being a limited partner of George Steinbrenner." I think McMullen might want to talk with a few Yankees managers and general managers before he starts talking in absolutes about being "limited" by the Boss.

On May 11, 1979, I was in San Francisco with the Philadelphia Phillies when the Yankees—in need of a left-hander in the bullpen—picked up my contract off of waivers. I took the red-eye to New York and went straight from the airport to the stadium. Bob Lemon was the manager (at that moment) and greeted me with, "Welcome to the Bronx Zoo. When can you pitch?"

I said, "I can pitch today if you need me." I came in that day to relieve Luis Tiant in the seventh inning with runners on first and third. I got my former teammate Rod Carew to ground into an inning-ending double play. I was officially a Yankee. Lemon had replaced Billy Martin in 1978 and helped guide the Yankees, who were 14 games back of the Red Sox, all the way to a second consecutive World Series title. But by June of '79 with the Yankees three games above .500, Steinbrenner fired Lemon and replaced him with the man he had replaced, Billy Martin. I'm in pinstripes a little over a month and already I'm experiencing the coaching carousel. Then in the offseason, Billy got into one of his famous fights, and he was out again, and Dick Howser was in. In less than a year, I had three different managers in the Bronx.

Martin managed the Yankees five different times because he did something that George absolutely loved: he lit fires under people. Billy began his pinstriped years as a second baseman in 1950 under legendary manager Casey Stengel. Billy was known as a clutch performer who won four championships in his first seven years in New York and was named World Series MVP in 1953. In 1957, while celebrating his 29th birthday at the famous Copacabana nightclub in Manhattan, Battlin' Billy led a contingent of six Yankees, including Mickey Mantle, Whitey Ford, and Yogi Berra in a bar fight. A month later Billy was traded to Kansas City. Many have said the trade was instigated by Billy's hard partying lifestyle, which was seen as a bad influence on Ford and Mantle. Once he left the Bronx, Billy played on six different teams in five years. I was a teammate of his on the last team he played for, the 1961 Twins. In one of Billy's first games with us, he hit a three-run home run, I pitched a complete game, and we ended a 12-game losing streak.

I also played under Martin in Minnesota back in 1969. I enjoyed

Manager Billy Martin (left) endured a love-hate relationship with owner George Steinbrenner, who hired and fired Martin five times.

playing for him because he let pitchers pitch. One time in Oakland, I was sent to the showers after only four innings in the first game of a double-header. I thought I just didn't have my usual stuff that day. In the second game, Billy comes to me and asks, "You got anything left, Kitty? Can you give me a couple of innings?" "Sure," I said. I ended up pitching again. I can't think of any manager today who would use a pitcher like that in two games in one day.

Billy had a habit of throwing his catchers under the bus and blaming them for any big hits by the other team. (That was never fun to see as a pitcher.) He also had a loose relationship with the truth. I was once chewed out by Twins owner Calvin Griffith because I had left the team to visit my father in the hospital between games. Billy had given me permission to go, but when Griffith asked him where I was, Martin said, "I guess he missed the flight home."

I will say this: Billy knew how to get every last drop of talent out of his players and how to get every advantage he could out of a situation. A great tactician, he was the epitome of the phrase "when you least expect it, expect it." He set a record with the Twins by having Rod Carew steal home seven times in a single season. He was a master of trick plays. Let's say you have runners on first and third, and the guy at first takes off for second but falls down halfway. Now he's caught in a rundown, but as the defense tries to tag him, the guy from third scores. Ever seen that one? It's pure Billy Martin.

Don Baylor tells the story of a game in 1985 against the Tigers. The score was tied with two runners on for New York, and lefty Mickey Mahler was on the mound for Detroit. Always looking for an edge, Billy tells third baseman Mike Pagliarulo to bat from the right side. Only Pags *isn't* a switch-hitter. He'd never hit other than from the left side his entire major league career. But he does what he is told. Baylor and the guys on the bench are sure Billy has something up his sleeve. They watch and wait for the trick to reveal itself. Pitch after pitch, they wait for Billy to spring the trap. Instead, Pags strikes out awkwardly, and the Yankees go on to lose the game. This time, there was no trick. Apparently, there was no method to his madness on this particular day.

Billy knew the rulebook inside and out, which was demonstrated during the infamous Pine Tar Game on July 24th, 1983 against the Kansas City Royals. Third baseman George Brett's ninth-inning home run was nullified, and Brett was called out because the pine tar on his bat exceeded 18 inches. An enraged Brett charging out of the visitor's dugout at umpire Tim McClelland is one of the more memorable images in baseball history, and it only happened because Billy was the one who brought it to the umpires' attention. Apparently, Billy had seen the excessive pine tar on Brett's bat months before but waited until it was strategically important to use that information. It resulted in a Yankees win…but only temporarily. The Royals protested the game, and American League president Lee MacPhail overruled McClelland, meaning Brett's home run counted, and the game would have to be resumed with two outs in the top of the ninth and the Royals leading 5–4. But since the umpiring crew was different in the resumed contest than in the first game, Billy tried to protest that Brett hadn't touched all the bases on his home run. That's when umpire Dave Phillips pulled out a signed affidavit from the original umpire crew that stated all runners had touched all bases. They *knew* Billy would try to pull something and had to get a notarized document to outflank the Yankees skipper.

In addition to his multiple Yankees stints, Billy managed five different teams. He seemed to have a knack for turning losers into winners, but he also seemed to struggle with sustaining those winners over longer stretches of time. Although his feuds with Steinbrenner were the stuff of legend, the two kept being drawn back to each other. Billy was working as a special assistant to George when he died in a car crash during a Christmas Day ice storm in 1989. On his headstone there is a quote from Martin, which he uttered at the retiring of his number at Yankee Stadium: "I may not have been the greatest Yankee to put on the uniform. But I was the proudest."

When Billy was fired the first time back in 1978, he had managed 471 games in a row for the Bombers. No manager would get close to that until Buck Showalter took over the top job in the Bronx in 1992. He would last four seasons and 582 games. Buck never made it to the majors as a player. He was a minor league first baseman in the Yankees organization during the Mattingly years. But Buck was a sharp cookie and he was manager of the Yankees at the ripe age of 35 after coaching in the minors for a few years. As young as he was, Buck was a student of the game. He loved Old Timers' Day and the history it brought to life. And it bothered him when his players didn't appreciate it. In a *Newsday* article, Buck admitted

MANAGERS DURING THE STEINBRENNER YEARS

January 3, 1973
George bought the team/
Ralph Houk manager

'73

September 30, 1973
Houk resigned

January 3, 1974
Bill Virdon hired

'74

August 1, 1975
Virdon fired/Billy Martin hired (1)

'75

October 18, 1977
Yanks win World Series (21)

'77

July 24, 1978
Martin resigned

July 25, 1978
Bob Lemon hired

'78

October 17, 1978
Yanks win World Series (22)

June 18, 1979
Lemon fired/Martin hired (2)

'79

October 28, 1979
Martin fired/Dick Howser hired

November 21, 1980
Howser resigned/Gene Michael hired

'80

September 6, 1981
Michael fired/Lemon hired (2)

'81

October 15, 1981
Yanks win AL Pennant (33)

April 26, 1982
Lemon fired/Michael hired (2)

August 3, 1982
Michael fired/Clyde King named
interim mgr

'82

January 11, 1983
Martin hired (3)

'83

December 16, 1983
Martin fired/Yogi Berra hired

April 28, 1985
Berra fired/Martin hired (4)

'85

October 27, 1985
Martin fired/Lou Piniella hired

October 19, 1987
Piniella promoted to GM/
Martin hired (5)

'87

June 23, 1988
Martin fired/Piniella hired (2)

'88

October 7, 1988
Piniella fired/Dallas Green hired

August 18, 1989
Green fired/Bucky Dent hired

'89

June 6, 1990
Dent fired/Stump Merrill hired

'90

October 7, 1991
Merrill fired

'91

October 29, 1991
Buck Showalter hired

October 26, 1995
Showalter resigned

'95

Novemebr 2, 1995
Joe Torre hired

October 26, 1996
Yanks win World Series (23)

'96

October 21, 1998
Yanks win World Series (24)

'98

October 27, 1999
Yanks win World Series (25)

'99

October 26, 2000
Yanks win World Series (26)

'00

October 22, 2001
Yanks win AL Pennant (38)

'01

October 16, 2003
Yanks win AL Pennant (39)

'03

October 18, 2007
Torre left

October 30, 2007
Joe Girardi hired

'07

November 4, 2009
Yanks win World Series (27)

'09

July 13, 2010
Steinbrenner died

'10

he made up his mind to trade a player when that player walked out of the dugout on Old Timers' Day and wondered, "Who are all these old guys?" Showalter said to himself, *I hope you enjoy Montreal next year.*

At first, Buck was a hard manager to cover. He was always on guard early in his career. He always seemed leery of divulging information or saying something wrong, and it made him come off as distant. But as time went on and I got to know him, he became a very enjoyable manager to talk to. The quality of managers today and the way they address questions is a lot different than when I was coming up. No longer is it the rough and gruff tobacco-chewing guys like Lemon or Martin, who swear and spit on the floor. Now you have Brad Ausmus from Dartmouth and Bob Melvin from Cal-Berkeley. Mike Scioscia has a computer science degree from Penn State for crying out loud. These well-educated and well-spoken managers will give you straight answers. Baseball has definitely changed.

Showalter fit in that vein and had a knack for building teams. During his stint in the Bronx, the Yankees ended their 13-year postseason drought in 1995. (He would've more than likely ended it a year earlier if not for the work stoppage in '94, the same year he was voted American League Manager of the Year.) In order to help build the team from the ground up, Buck became the first manager in the history of the expansion Arizona Diamondbacks in 1996, two years before they would play a game. It worked. He led the D-backs to the second best record in the National League and into the playoffs in just their second season. But like with the Yankees, he was let go after early success. Buck's ability to construct winners has led to an unfortunate distinction. In both New York and Arizona, he was fired the year before the teams—that he helped build—won the World Series.

As tough as it was being a manager for Steinbrenner, being a general manager was no picnic either. Steinbrenner employed 11 GMs over his 30-plus years with the team. A big part of the GM's job during those years was keeping George from inflicting damage to his own team. And nobody knows how hard that can be more than Bob Watson.

At the end of the 1997 season, Steinbrenner fell in love with the idea of landing Chuck Knoblauch. The Yankees had won their first title in 18 years the season before only to see that year's team rot from the inside out. Several players who did all they could for the team in '96 were out for themselves in '97, and the Yankees didn't repeat. That only fed George's desire for another title. One player he thought would help achieve that was Minnesota's second baseman.

Chuck had just been named an All-Star, and Watson was well aware that his asking price would be too steep for the Twins to re-sign him. After all, major league negotiations are a high stakes game of poker, and if you are good at it, you can tell when the other team is bluffing. Minnesota's first response to inquiries for Knoblauch was to say it would cost New York Bernie Williams *and* Andy Pettitte. That was an absurdly high asking price, but it was simply a way to skew the negotiations higher. When they came down to highly touted infield prospect Cristian Guzman and first-round left hander Eric Milton, it sounded reasonable to George. But Watson wouldn't do the deal. He told George that if the Yankees waited, there was a good chance they'd get Chuck for "two broken fungo bats and a bag of BP balls" because the Twins didn't have much in the way of options. But George couldn't wait and ordered Watson to make the trade. Watson, who saw it as his job to protect the franchise—even from the owner, refused. George said the deal would get done with or without him. So Bob resigned.

Another great Yankees GM was Gene Michael, whom everybody called "Stick." Gene and I go back to his playing days. He was a shortstop for the Yankees from 1968–1974. He could tag a base runner out as quickly as anybody I've ever seen. It was a very helpful skill to have on close calls at second base. Gene was a slick fielder but not a very potent hitter. He loves the game, loves scouting and talent evaluating, and is very respected by his peers. Stick managed the Yankees and the Chicago Cubs for a few years each in the '80s and became a very influential baseball man, one of the few voices that could sway George on player decisions. Coming out of spring training in '96, there was a discussion about the future of Derek Jeter. He did not have a particularly good spring, and George was getting nervous about starting a rookie at short. Watson wanted to let the kid start the season. Former GM Clyde King thought they should send Jeter down to Triple A Columbus and trade for a more established player. Clyde seemed to be steering Steinbrenner that way until Stick stepped in. Gene, who was also a former GM and who was then scouting for the club, said to King about the young shortstop, "You seem to forget I *played* the position. And this kid is better than I ever was." Gene convinced George to let Jeter learn on the job and not do anything until the All-Star break. It turned out to be a very good idea.

In 1986 the Yankees hired a young man as an intern. Stick took a liking to this guy and took him under his wing. So did Watson. So when Bob resigned, he made sure to suggest this guy as his replacement. That's when a 30-year-old former intern, Brian Cashman, got the top job. Cashman, who was previously the assistant GM, was at the helm as senior vice president and general manager through the championship years of the late 1990s and 2009. He relied heavily on what he learned from the old guard and the system they had built up. He was an unproven choice back in '98, but history has shown he did not disappoint.

Broadway Joe

Another man who did not disappoint was Joseph Paul Torre. A lot of people forget that Torre was a heck of a ballplayer in his day. He won a Gold Glove as a catcher in 1965 and the batting crown and NL MVP in '71 as a third baseman. In the nine All-Star Games he was in, he earned starting spots at both catcher and third base. His head for the

Prior to a 2004 game, I hang out with Joe Torre, who led the Yankees to four World Series titles.

game was evident early on as the Mets named him a player-manager in May of 1977 at the age of 36. Joe never made it to the postseason in 18 years as a player. And in his 14 years of managing before coming to the Bronx, he got there only once—with the '82 Atlanta Braves. In fact, at that point in his career, Joe had a terrible bit of trivia attached to his name. No one in baseball history had ever played and/or managed more games without reaching the World Series than Joe Torre. No wonder the New York press greeted his hiring with headlines like "Clueless Joe." But the Brooklyn-born Torre and his even-keel approach were a perfect fit for Steinbrenner's Yankees. Joe led the team to the postseason in every one of his 12 seasons in New York. And when he left the team in 2007, neither Casey Stengel nor even Miller Huggins could match his longevity in the Bronx. Only the great Joe McCarthy can say he managed the Yankees longer than Joe Torre.

Joe took over the Yankees in 1996 in the wake of the team's crushing loss in the 1995 American League Divison Series to the Seattle Mariners.

Since that October collapse, manager Buck Showalter and general manager Gene Michael were relieved of their duties, and Don Mattingly, the face of the franchise, had retired. I'm not sure Joe knew what he was getting into, but he knew who he was going to ride to get there. It would be on the shoulders of a 22-year-old rookie shortstop and a 26-year-old starter-turned-reliever.

A turning point in Yankees history came in 1996. So it only seems fitting that the Yankees' first trip to the World Series in 15 years *turned* on one of the most memorable plays of the 20th century. It came in Game 1 of the American League Championship Series. The Yankees were hosting a powerful Baltimore club. That season the Orioles hit 257 home runs, the most ever by a franchise in a single season in baseball history up until that point. (The Mariners would hit 264 the very next season. The Yankees record is 242 in 2004, which is two more than the team with Maris and Mantle hit in 1961.) In the bottom of the eighth inning, the score was 4–3 in favor of Baltimore when Derek Jeter stepped up to the plate. Derek had had a pretty good rookie campaign, hitting .314 with 10 home runs and 78 RBIs. But what impressed Torre and everyone around the ballclub was how poised this kid was. And how the big moment didn't seem to faze him. On the contrary, it seemed to excite him. And on that chilly October afternoon, a big moment hung in the air when Derek sent the first pitch from Armando Benitez deep to right field.

Baltimore had put Tony Tarasco into right field as a defensive replacement, and he drifted back to the wall, tracking the ball all the way. At the same time, 12-year-old Jeffrey Maier was hopping out of Seat 2 in Row A, Box 325 in Section 31 and heading straight to the railing doing exactly the same thing. Both Maier and Tarasco put up their gloves. The next thing Torre saw was right-field umpire Rich Garcia signal home run. The Yankees had tied it. Then he saw Tarasco, then Benitez, then Orioles manager Davey Johnson get in Garcia's face. Johnson would get tossed, and the home run would stand. It was the first postseason homer of Jeter's career, but replays clearly showed that Maier reached out over into the field of play to touch the ball. He didn't actually catch it. The ball hit off the heel of his glove and caromed over the wall to be eventually corralled by a 35-year-old Connecticut man named Marc Jarvis. Dave Schoenfield of ESPN would later call Garcia's gaffe the worst umpiring call in baseball history. The Yanks would go on to win the game 5–4 on an 11th inning home run by Bernie Williams. As for Torre, who was inundated after the game with questions about the Yankees winning unfairly and the undeniable video evidence in support, he gave a pitch-perfect response: "Anyone see a replay of Bernie's home run? That wasn't bad either." Joe cleverly pointed out that the Maier play didn't win the game. The deal was still there to be closed by either team, but it was Torre's Yankees who did it.

Torre had another great moment off the field during that postseason. After the Yankees dropped the first two games of the World Series to the defending champion Braves by a combined score of 16–1, Joe made a bold yet confident prediction to his team and Steinbrenner. He said the Yankees were going to go into Atlanta and win three in a row and then come back to New York to take Game 6. It seemed like folly at the time, but Joe explained, "Atlanta's my town." What many don't know is that Torre had actually told Steinbrenner that the Yankees would *lose* Game 2 to Greg Maddux in the Bronx before winning the next four. I know George well enough to know that took a lot of guts for a first-year manager to say. But perhaps because Game 2 played out as he expected, Torre was confident in the ultimate result of the series. And he was correct. The man who had never been to the Fall Classic looked like he had invented the darn thing. He was part Stengel, part Nostradamus.

Joe had to navigate many highs and lows during his time as skipper. Torre's oldest brother, Rocco, a former New York City policeman, died suddenly during Joe's first season in the Bronx. He responded by throwing himself deeper into the game. Another big brother, Frank, a former major league ballplayer who won a title with the Milwaukee Braves in 1957 *against* the Yankees, had successful heart transplant surgery the night before the '96 Yankees beat the Atlanta Braves to win it all. When people saw Joe crying with the trophy, they thought those tears were for finally achieving his World Series dream. But in reality they were for his family and for everything they went through to get Joe to this point.

Joe's 1998 team won a then-AL-record 114 regular season games and has to be considered alongside the 1927 Murderer's Row and the 1961 Maris and Mantle squads as one of the all-time best teams in Yankees history. (Managed by former Yankee Lou Piniella, the Mariners had two more victories in '01, tying the 1906 Chicago Cubs for the major league record of 116.) Joe had his own health issues as well, missing 35 games in 1999 when he was treated for prostate cancer.

Don Zimmer skippered the club in Joe's absence, going 21–15 during that time. It's hard to talk about Torre without mentioning Zimmer. The two were very close. Zim was one of my favorite people in baseball as well. Don was always a straight shooter and told it like it was, even if that meant he was to blame. That infamous brawl with Pedro Martinez of the Red Sox during the 2003 ALCS, when Pedro put a charging Zimmer on the ground was a case in point. It was Game 3 in Boston. After a Roger Clemens pitch over the head of Manny Ramirez, the benches cleared. In the middle of the chaos, Zimmer charged Pedro, who basically threw the 72-year-old man to the ground. Clearly tempers were still hot the next day, and everyone in New York wanted to bury Martinez. Everyone that is—except Zimmer. He was deeply embarrassed by it and apologized to the Yankees and their fans, as well as the Red Sox and their fans, during a press conference. As he said years later, "I was definitely wrong, and Pedro didn't do nothing." It takes a big man to admit that in the middle of one of the most heated rivalries in all of sports.

Zim also helped make the game a little safer, but he did it the hard way. Back in his playing days, he was with the Brooklyn Dodgers' minor league affiliate in St. Paul, Minnesota, when he was hit in the head by a pitch. Zim would be unconscious for nearly two weeks and had holes drilled in his skull to relieve pressure. He returned to baseball and won a ring with the '55 Dodgers, but his career was never the same. Then, as the Yankees bench coach he was hit by a foul ball off the bat of Chuck Knoblauch in the opening game of the playoff series with the Texas Rangers in 1999. He only suffered a few cuts and returned to the bench for the rest of the game after some treatment. The next game Zimmer was back on the bench, only this time with an army helmet that had the Yankees logo and "ZIM" painted on it. That incident led the Yankees to install mesh fences in front of the dugout to protect players and coaches from shots like Knoblauch's. Those fences are now seen on dugouts throughout baseball.

Zimmer left the Yankees in 2003, another acrimonious split courtesy of Steinbrenner. Some date the start of the rift back to when Zim filled in as manager during Torre's cancer treatment. George had called a meeting of his coaches and began it by saying, "Anyone who thinks they are doing the best job they can right now can get up and leave." So Don got up and left. George was dumbfounded that someone took him up on his statement. I'm sure Don thought, *If you don't mean it, don't say it.* When Joe came back, George never thanked Zim, publicly or privately, for the job he did in Torre's absence. I think that snub burned Zim and just greased the skids for the eventual split. The day the Yankees lost to the Marlins in the 2003 World Series, Zim said he had had enough of Steinbrenner, and he was out of there. And being a man of his word, he was. He ended up hooking up with the Devil Rays and stayed with them until he passed away in 2014 at the age of 83. When he died, Zim was the last active Major League Baseball person to play for the Brooklyn Dodgers.

Torre was also there for the return of Yogi Berra to the Yankees family. That led to a funny spring training story. The Yankees had an away game not too far from their Tampa facilities so Joe, as he often did, drove his coaches to the game. He's got Zimmer, Mattingly, and Yogi all in the car driving along when Yogi says he needs to use the facilities. So they pull into a gas station and out hops Yogi—in full uniform, mind you, cleats and all—and goes off to find the men's room. Zim and Don decide they might as well use it, too, so they go in. Can you imagine what the store clerk must've thought, seeing all of this Yankees history clacking through his store to the men's room?

The thing that always impressed me about Torre was his ability to do the press conferences every day and answer the same questions from the same people. I felt very privileged. Having a personal relationship with Joe, I could get the answers I wanted about his team. And how he trusted that I wouldn't say anything over the air that was personal and confidential.

In 2007 Joe became the answer to a much better bit of trivia: who was the first man in baseball to earn 2,000 wins as a manager and have 2,000 hits as a player? *I'll take "Joe Torre" for $1,000, Alex.* But that was also Joe's last year in New York. After all he did to return the Yankees to their glory days, Steinbrenner offered a contract that cut Torre's base salary and looked more like the incentive-laden deal you offer an unproven rookie manager, not Torre. Joe passed on the deal, and on October 18th, 2007, the Torre era in New York came to a close. It was a sorry way to end a terrific run. But there are few graceful exits in sports. It's the nature of the beast, I guess. Joe went on to coach the Los Angeles Dodgers for three years before taking a job with Major League Baseball as an executive vice president for baseball operations. In July of 2014, Joe was inducted into the Hall of Fame along with fellow managers Tony La Russa and Bobby Cox.

That honor is very deserving. Joe was a great leader, something perhaps best demonstrated during the toughest days for anyone involved in the Yankees organization—the 9/11 attacks. It was a time unlike any other in history of New York, and the entire Yankees organization rose to the occasion.

CHAPTER 9
A SEASON FOR THE CITY

There are many remarkable moments in Yankees history. Some were before my time in uniform: Ruth calling his shot, DiMaggio's 56-game hitting streak, Don Larsen's perfect game in the World Series. Others I vividly remember: Maris and Mantle in '61, Reggie in October, Bucky in Boston, Aaron Boone's shot in '03, Derek being Derek plenty of times. But in my humble opinion, the finest moment in Yankees history during my watch—and perhaps ever—wasn't really a moment. And it didn't end in victory. It was the first time since the Babe put on pinstripes that the ultimate goal of the Yankees season wasn't to win a title. It was something a lot more meaningful...and a lot harder to do. Somehow the New York Yankees managed to help pull a city from the abyss and turn what could've been the darkest days in the history of the franchise into its finest hour.

September 11, 2001, was one of those events in history—like the assassination of President Kennedy—that those of us who are old enough will always remember where we were when it happened. I was riding my bike around my neighborhood in St. Petersburg, Florida, when JFK was shot. I was sitting in my apartment on New York's Upper East Side with my late wife, MaryAnn, when my daughter called me from New Jersey and said a plane had hit the World Trade Center and to turn on the TV. I didn't need the TV. I could just look out the window and see the smoke billowing into the sky all the way from 65th Street. And then came the thousands of people walking up 3rd Avenue to get as far away from the scene as possible. Many of the players talked about seeing dazed, soot-covered people making their way up town, almost like zombies, just trying to get to the safety of their homes. No trains or buses were running. People who had spent their entire lives in the city found themselves walking from one borough to the next for the first time in their lives. My wife and I walked down a block to the blood bank, and the line was winding all the way around the corner from 66th Street onto 2nd Avenue. We were glad to see so many of our neighbors had the same desire to help. Unfortunately, most of us were turned away. It turned out blood wasn't needed. There weren't enough survivors. Derek Jeter left his apartment that afternoon. He thought the scene outside was like a movie set, like something out of the Will Smith film, *I Am Legend*. The greatest city in the world, the city that never sleeps, was suddenly devoid of everyday life in the middle of the day.

It was a terrible day that quickly became the first of many bad days. Nothing was the same. And every time you looked downtown and saw that big gap in the skyline, it reminded you that thousands of people lost their lives. Several members of the Yankees family, people who worked for years in the organization selling tickets or working with fans, lost loved ones on that day. Everyone knew somebody who was directly affected.

The New York Mets and Yankees both stepped up to help. Both organizations made public and private donations to the cause. But it was hard to know the right way to go about helping. The Yankees front office organized some trips by the players to firehouses and police stations to thank those first responders for the job they were doing. These guys were working round the clock shifts in those first few weeks, so to give them a lighter moment during those heavy days was important. Some in the organization thought it would be good to publicize these visits by having the papers there. The hope was people who were basically shell-shocked and not doing anything might think, *Hey, the Yankees are getting out there to do something. Maybe I should go down and cheer up the firemen on my block, bring them some lasagna or cookies or something.* But others, including Jeter, felt it was better to show up unannounced without the press around. That's what usually happened. After a knock at the firehouse door, in walked four or five of the Yankees to say thanks for all that they were doing. The stories got out anyway.

A Captain's Tribute On the eight-year anniversary of 9/11, the Yankees played the Baltimore Orioles at Yankee Stadium. After a moment of silent remembrance to those lost and other tributes to the survivors, Derek Jeter went out and passed Lou Gehrig on the all-time Yankees hit list. A single in the third gave him 2,722 and pushed him past the Iron Horse. It seemed fitting in a way that the ultimate team player would claim a career milestone on a day when much of the focus was not on him or his remarkable achievement but on others.

Some of the Yankees players left to be with their families. Roger Clemens drove all the way to Texas. On Saturday, September 15, the Yankees chartered some vans to take a dozen or so players and coaches including Jeter, Scott Brosius, and Bernie Williams, as well as Joe Torre and Don Zimmer, into Manhattan. Their first stop was the Javits Center over on 11th Avenue, right where the Lincoln Tunnel comes into Manhattan from New Jersey. That was a staging area for volunteers and rescue workers. The players walked around and met these people from all over the tri-state area and beyond coming in to help. Some knew people who had been lost; others just couldn't sit by and do nothing. Most were exhausted from the grueling and dangerous work. Many of the volunteers asked for autographs. One asked to rub Zimmer's head for good luck—like Derek would do sometimes. The players all signed without hesitation, but afterward Jeter thought it should've been the other way around—that the players should be asking these guys and gals for their autographs.

Then they went up to the Park Avenue Armory. This was where people gathered to await news of missing family members. By this point there was very little if any good news coming out of Ground Zero. Torre described it as "heart-wrenching." But the Yankees wanted to give these poor people something—anything—to smile about, even if it was just for a minute. Williams met an older woman who was hoping to hear about a loved one. Bernie is the sweetest guy you could ever meet, but, like all the Yankees, he was struggling with what to say and how to act. So he walked up to this lady he never met before and said, "You look like you need a hug." And he hugged her. She cried in his arms.

It was emotionally tough for the ballplayers, but it was what New Yorkers needed. Paul O'Neill was asked to spend a half hour with the family members of victims. Twelve hours later he was still there. A young boy, who had been crying, handed Paul a Beanie Baby for him to autograph. As he did, the kid looked down at the cast on O'Neill's foot. When he got his Beanie Baby back, the kid said to Paul, "Thanks. And I hope your foot feels better." Paul learned that boy had lost one of his parents, and *he* was the one wishing O'Neill well.

Baseball was shut down. Commissioner Bud Selig suspended games across the entire league for a week after the attack. He hadn't forgotten that former NFL commissioner Pete Rozelle always said his biggest mistake was not suspending all games the Sunday after President Kennedy's assassination. It was hard to know what to do in the days afterward. Baseball seemed like such a trivial thing to do when people were still searching for loved ones in the rubble at Ground Zero and the Pentagon. But after the initial shock of the attack, life *did* have to get back to normal. Otherwise the terrorists would be getting more of what they wanted from the attack—to ruin our way of life.

Play was set to resume on September 17. The Yankees had a game in Chicago the next day. When we got back to our jobs of announcing, we really started seeing the outpouring of support for New York. It was very emotional. We were the visiting team at Comiskey Park, and yet the organ played, "New York, New York." And there were banners saying, "We Love NY" being held by White Sox fans. When the team took the field, the (usually hated) Yankees received a standing ovation from the

221

Chicago crowd. It was something I never expected to see in my lifetime. It was a wonderful example of American unity.

The team played three games in Chicago and then three in Baltimore. While playing six games in six days, the Yankees went 3–3. Then they headed back to the Bronx to face the Devil Rays on the 25th. By this time the Mets had already played the first game in the city since the attacks. On September 21 Mike Piazza lifted the Mets over the Atlanta Braves 3–2 with a tremendous home run in the bottom of the eighth inning at Shea Stadium. For the Yankees' first game, the most chilling moment was listening to Daniel Rodriguez sing "God Bless America." I think all of us in the booth were swallowing hard, and our voices were cracking a little bit after that. The game might have been too much emotionally for the team as well. The Rays shut out the Yankees 4–0 that night.

The Yankees were comfortably in first place of the American League East on September 10. They continued to play well through that fall. I remember seeing mayor Rudy Giuliani and his son at the stadium a lot that fall. It was a way to tell people it was okay to come back out and gather in public spaces. For the first five months of the season, the mantra for the three-time defending champions was "Four in a Row." But now the plan had changed. Now the driving force didn't seem to be a title. It was to do whatever it takes to extend their season, to play as long as they could into the fall to take New Yorkers' minds off of the devastation at the heart of their city, to give people with nothing to smile about a reason—however brief—to smile. That was the goal. And if you went down to Ground Zero at night in late October, every now and then you'd hear a cheer erupt. It would be for the Yankees winning another game. It really picked up spirits. Scott Brosius noticed another difference. For the rest of the season, he said, "We weren't the hated Yankees. We were the symbol for what these people in New York were going through." There was a time there where every game felt a little bit like a home game.

> **Yogi to the Rescue** Tourism is a huge part of the New York City economy. Months after 9/11, New York called on some of its favored sons and daughters to help tell people the city was safe to visit. Robert De Niro, Billy Crystal, Woody Allen, Barbara Walters, and Christopher Walken all did video spots for the New York Miracle campaign. But my favorite was always Yogi's. He's seen conducting an orchestra in tux and tails before asking, "Who in the heck is this guy, Phil Harmonic?"

When the playoffs rolled around, the pressure only increased. The players were always welcoming firemen and policemen or meeting the families of victims as they were preparing to play. Brosius remembered crying five minutes before a game started because he couldn't help but feel their pain. At some point being the emotional lift for a city of 10 million gets to be an emotional drain. The Yankees lost the first two games to the Oakland A's, the AL's wild-card. There were not as many cheers heard down at Ground Zero. But the Yankees rallied for their town. Game 3 brought Jeter's famous flip play. That play by itself got plenty of minds off of the grueling work being done at the southern end of Manhattan. The Yankees took Game 4 as well and were back in the Bronx to close out the A's.

I remember Phil Rizzuto kicked things off that night with a piece of theater inspired by Jeter. Scooter was throwing out the first pitch and he smuggled an extra ball out to the mound. After tossing the ceremonial first pitch as planned, Scooter walked toward the dugout. He got to just about where Derek had made his famous flip in Oakland and Scooter pulls out this other ball and flips it to Yankees utility man Clay Bellinger. The crowd went wild. Derek would have his second great play—the dive into the photobox—of that series. He made the out, climbed back on to the field, and played the rest of the game, but that play definitely took more out of D.J. than he let on. But with all these other people hurting so much more, he never said a thing.

Next up were the Seattle Mariners. My old Yankees teammate, Lou Piniella, led Seattle to not only the best record in baseball that season, but the also best ever—116 wins in the regular season. With the Mariners sparked by Japanese superstar Ichiro Suzuki in his rookie season, many thought that New York had stretched this run as far as they could. Instead the Yankees took the first two in Seattle before coming home to close the deal in five games. Andy Pettitte won Games 1 and 5, and Alfonso Soriano hit a two-run, bottom of the ninth homer to win Game 4. The biggest thing about this series was how the support of the team and the city became a real two-way street. Just like the Yankees were picking up the spirits of the rescue workers, now the fans were picking up the spirits of the Yankees. Torre always knew that Yankee Stadium was a special place, but even he never felt it like this. That season, he said, "We just feel the heartbeat of the people."

The Yankees made it to their fourth straight World Series. Even Yogi Berra was impressed. The Bronx Bombers would take their 26 championships and decades of history up against a franchise that was still in diapers. The Arizona Diamondbacks were only in their fourth season but had been built from the ground up by former Yankees manager Buck Showalter, and he knew what he was doing. Though Bob Brenly assumed the reins for the World Series run, Showalter helped the D-backs get to the Fall Classic faster than any franchise in history—with great pitching and a lot of veterans who had never won a title. So they were hungry. The one thing they didn't have was the country behind them. Usually, if your team doesn't make the series, you root for the underdog. The Yankees had won the last three titles, and they were the Yankees. But this year it was hard for anyone to root against them.

Arizona would win the first two games in the desert behind their one-two pitching punch of Curt Schilling and Randy Johnson. Just like that, the Yankees were on the ropes again. At least they were coming back home to New York. But even though it was at home, things were different for Game 3. President Bush was going to be there to throw out the first pitch. In a season full of firsts, now the players had to deal with bomb-sniffing dogs around their lockers. Bush, of course, was a baseball man, having been managing general partner of the Texas Rangers for six years. He wanted to project an image of confidence and strength by firing a strike in front of the entire country. But he had to have on a bulletproof vest under the FDNY jacket he was wearing. He was practicing throwing from the base of the mound in the batting cages under the stadium when Jeter walked up. The Yankees shortstop wanted to know if the president was going to throw in front of the mound or from on top. Bush said he was leaning toward in front. Derek said it'd be better from the mound. As the president tried a few throws from the practice mound, Derek headed back to the locker room. But before he left, he gave the president of the United States one last piece of advice: "Don't bounce it. This is New York. They'll boo you." That's what I love about Derek—the unflinching confidence to tell the president what others around him probably knew but didn't have the guts to say.

Bush threw his strike and left to chants of "USA, USA." Clemens then threw a bunch of them, and the Yankees left with a 2–1 victory. The next game they were up against it again. Trailing 3–1 with a man on and down to their final out in the bottom of the ninth inning, Tino Martinez stepped in against Byung-Hyun Kim, the Arizona closer. Tino remembered Kim had thrown him a bunch of fastballs before switching to his slider in a previous game. So he guessed fastball and swung at the first pitch he saw and put it over the wall to tie the score. It was an October shot worthy of Reggie Jackson. The victory, however, would have to wait until the following month.

Because baseball shut down after the attacks on September 11, this was the latest World Series in history. Game 4 was played on Halloween. So while Jeter was in the batter's box in the bottom of the 10th inning, the clock struck midnight, and the calendar flipped the page. Derek then hit the first World Series home run in the month of November. It was also the first walk-off of Derek's career. Not a bad time to check that one off the list. These Yankees were not only winning, but they were also doing it with style.

That trend continued the next game as well when the Yankees were again down by two in the bottom of the ninth inning. This time it was Brosius taking Kim out of the yard to tie the game at two. When Soriano knocked in Chuck Knoblauch in the bottom of the 12th, a remarkable feat repeated itself. Never before in World Series history had a team with two out in the bottom of the ninth hit a game-tying home run and gone on to win the game. The Yankees had just done it on back-to-back nights. The Yankees were definitely the story that fall in New York. They continued to take their fans to the brink and back, keeping their full attention until the wee hours of the morning.

The team headed west with a 3–2 lead and high hopes of completing their run to a 27th title. Game 6 was at Bank One Ballpark in Arizona. Andy Pettitte was the starter. He'd lost Game 2 to Randy Johnson, but Pettitte was also the MVP of the American League Championship Series. Andy would end his career as the all-time league leader in post-season wins with 19. He's also the only pitcher in baseball history to play in at least 18 seasons without ever posting a losing record. He was a big-game performer. But this day the D-backs spotted something in Andy's windup that tipped his pitches, so the hitters knew what was coming. Former Cy Young winner Rick Sutcliffe saw it, too. He was on the international broadcast for Game 6 and never said what it was that he saw, but he successfully predicted a series of pitches, so Andy was definitely giving away something. After the first two batters of the game, Arizona had a 1–0 lead. Andy would give up three more in the second and he was gone after a walk and double to start the third inning. The Diamondbacks would roll in this one 15–2.

As bad as this loss was, it also meant that the season would be

Before Game 5 of the 2001 World Series, which took place less than two months after 9/11, Derek Jeter wears a hat to honor the rescue workers.

extended one more time. Game 7 took place on November 4—two days shy of eight weeks removed from the worst attack on American soil. By this time several of the Yankees were feeling the drain of this unusual postseason. Like the city he was playing for, Jeter was hurting. That dive into the stands during the American League Division Series had left him a shell of himself. But the Yankees found the guts to rally once again in the seventh inning when Tino drove in Jeter. With the score tied 1–1 in the top of the eighth, Zimmer was talking about getting Mariano in to pitch the bottom of the eighth. But Joe Torre didn't want to bring Rivera in with the game tied—only with a lead. He thought things would be much simpler if Alfonso Soriano just hit a home run. And on an 0–2 pitch, that's exactly what he did.

That solved the problem of who would pitch the eighth. Mariano was a perfect 23–0 in postseason save opportunities. He came in and struck out the side in the bottom of the eighth inning. Destiny seemed to be wearing pinstripes. But in the ninth, the Yankees' magic ran out. The crucial play was a bunt fielded by Rivera. When he wheeled to throw to Jeter at second, the throw tailed like one of his pitches. The ailing Jeter did his best to snare it, but it was beyond the abilities of his battered body. Mariano would break three Arizona bats that inning, and all three went for hits, including the final bloop single over the drawn-in infield by Luis Gonzalez. As the D-backs celebrated their first title in the desert, the Yankees ran past them and into the clubhouse. The team hadn't lost a World Series since 1981. Jeter had never lost one. But if there ever was a time when it was okay to come up empty handed, it was 2001. As Mayor Giuliani said as he hugged George Steinbrenner, "Everyone in New York appreciates what you guys did for us."

If the Yankees had swept their way to victory that year, capturing the title in the minimum 11 games, I'm sure that would've made plenty of New Yorkers happy. But what the city needed more than a title that year was a distraction. And the Yankees definitely provided that for as long as they could. For me, it was a period of time in my life I will never forget. All New Yorkers, including myself, wondered how this tragedy could happen to the greatest city in the world. Looking back with years of perspective, maybe it happened there because that was the city that could handle it and still thrive. The Yankees definitely played a big part in that.

During those dark early days all the way through to Game 7 of the World Series that fall, Torre led the way. He set the tone that the entire organization followed. And he always seemed to find these little things that made a major impact on the team and in turn the city. Yankees games that fall were a chance for New Yorkers to cheer for something again, to find a brief moment when it was okay to be happy amidst all the devastation. The longer the Yankees played, the longer that excuse for happiness lasted.

During the fall months, Joe had worn an NYPD hat instead of a Yankees hat as a tribute to the first responders. But after New York had lost the first two games at home against the Oakland A's in the ALDS, it seemed the run was coming to an end. So now the team needed something else, a subtle nudge to remind them what they were playing for and to believe in themselves. So Joe asked Yogi for one of his "It Ain't Over Til It's Over" hats and had the NYPD letters stitched into the side. He began wearing that, and it more than did the trick. The Yankees had their backs against the wall several times that postseason and rallied time and time again. The hat finally lost its magic at the very end, but it helped give millions of New Yorkers a few more months of something to cheer about. It was things like that that made Joe special.

There are still echoes of that 2001 season at Yankee Stadium. The Yankees used to play "Take Me Out To the Ballgame" during the seventh-inning stretch. After 9/11, it has been "God Bless America." It's a small but constant reminder that the game of baseball has a bigger part to play in who we are as Americans and for what this nation ultimately represents.

EPILOGUE
TIP OF THE CAP

After 12 seasons as a Yankees broadcaster, I decided to hang up my microphone and retire in 2006. When I told my sister, Mildred, her first reaction was: "Retire from what? You never worked a day in your life." The truth is—she's right. I learned at an early age there were two things that I loved and that I was good at: throwing a baseball and talking in front of people. Somehow this kid from Zeeland, Michigan, was able to string together 58 years of people paying me to do those things that I loved. While I worked hard to improve myself in both areas every day I was doing them, I never thought of it as work. But as much as I loved baseball, family always came first.

I met MaryAnn Montanaro in 1986, and two years later she traded in the last name Montanaro for Kaat. She was born in New York but went to school and raised a family in Wisconsin. We both had grown children by then, so we were at the same place in life. She had been a fashion designer, but later in my career, MaryAnn became my agent. I used to be with a guy named Ed Hookstratten. But I learned that Ed was rude and unprofessional in his dealings with WCCO in Minneapolis for my contract in 1994, and we parted ways. When it came time to negotiate my deal with MSG Network in 1995, I was contacted by Mike McCarthy. Mike and his entire staff were always great to work with and were always supportive.

Mike thought he'd be talking to Hookstratten, but I told him I was now represented by MaryAnn Montanaro and that he should call her instead. Mike didn't know she was my wife. MaryAnn could be a real pit bull when it came to these sort of things and she proceeded to negotiate a very nice contract for me. Afterward Mike said to me, "This MaryAnn is pretty tough. I wish you were still represented by 'Hook.'" Late in 2004 MaryAnn was diagnosed with bladder cancer. She went through the painful treament process, and it went into remission. But we decided that it was time for me to step away from baseball. We wanted to take a year to travel around and see this great country of ours. After watching that thoughtful and humbling video that George Steinbrenner and the Yankees had put together about me and my career up there on the Jumbotron and throwing out that first pitch of that Red Sox-Yankees game that September, I stepped away from the game so MaryAnn and I could hit the road. And I wouldn't have traded those years for anything.

In April of 2008, the cancer returned. We headed back to Ripon, Wisconsin, to be with her family. On July 21st, in the house where she raised her kids and where her son still lived, MaryAnn passed away. It was a little over a week after Bobby Murcer died. That, to say the least, was a very tough summer for me.

When I retired I never really planned on announcing again. But in January of 2009, MLB Network launched. My old buddy, Tim McCarver, said I should get back in the game. So did Russ Gabay at MLB International. He called and asked if I'd do the World Baseball Classic that year down in Puerto Rico. It took some doing, but Russ convinced me to get back into broadcasting. So I did the WBC, and the next thing I knew, I got a call from the president and CEO of MLB Network, Tony Petitti. He asked, "Kitty, how would you like to do some games with Bob Costas?" *Bob Costas? Are you kidding me? What base-ball player-turned-analyst wouldn't want to do that?* Bob is an avid fan, an award-winning announcer, and just about the easiest guy to sit next to and talk baseball. I could not believe my good fortune. However, out of respect for how long I had announced Yankees games on MSG and YES, I thought the right thing to do was call John Filippelli and let him know that I was thinking about coming back and announcing a limited number of MLB games each year.

I know we had our differences, but when I retired, John did give me a contract that paid me a small sum so I could keep my health benefits. I thought that was a nice gesture and I made my appreciation known to Mr. Filippelli on several occasions. And I always enjoyed the people I worked with at YES Network. They were as professional as they could be and super to work with. Michael Kay went from a print media guy to a famous TV and radio personality. It was fun to have former players like Paul O'Neill, David Cone, Joe Girardi, John Flaherty, and Al Leiter begin their TV careers in the Yankees booth. I loved my time with Bobby Murcer and did my last games with him and Ken Singleton. "Singy" and I worked games—just the two of us—in the booth for over five years and found a very comfortable style, one that always got very nice support from the TV viewers. No one knew who was doing play-by-play and who was the analyst. We were just two former players talking baseball. It was seamless. I thought that maybe Mr. Filippelli would want to have that scenario again for the fans. The answer I got from him was there were "budgetary concerns." I assured him that money was not going to be an issue. I wanted to stay involved with the game and thought this was a good way to do it. When I heard back this time, he said that they had a full team of new analysts and the schedule was full. Sorry, no room for me on Yankees broadcasts. So I called Tony back at MLB Network, and it was the best thing that could have happened to me at that point in my life. 2014 was my sixth year here. I'm 76 now and consider myself so fortunate to be able to continue to do this. I don't say this to the guy I make my deals with, but to me this business is like legalized robbery. I'm getting paid to sit next to good friends and talk baseball like we are a couple of fans at the ballpark. The only things missing are the beer and peanuts. It's a pretty darn nice way to make a living.

Yankees fans are some of the most knowledgeable in the game, and I always enjoy running into one. They also ask me great questions about the team, about the game back then, about the game now. I am still amazed at the amount of times at either a baseball memorabilia show or a speaking engagement or just on the streets that I get stopped by people who say, "We sure miss you on the Yankees games," "You and Kenny were such a pleasure to listen to," or "We learned a lot about baseball from you and Kenny." It is very satisfying to hear that what you say on the air is meaningful to the viewer. Because, even though we are employed by the networks, we really work for the fams. So if you were one of those Yankees fans wondering why I never came back to do a few games in the Bronx, now you know. It wasn't because I didn't try.

No matter what, I thoroughly enjoyed my time in New York. The Yankees are more than a logo with the interlocking NY. They are a group of people driven to put the best product possible on the field. It was all fostered by George. Brian Cashman, Jean Afterman, Lonn Trost, Debbie Tymon, and many more office personnel became friends.

It was a surreal moment for me in 2008. As the list of the Yankees family members who passed away was scrolling on the Jumbotron at Old Timers' Day, I saw the name "MaryAnn Kaat" up there. That meant a lot. We really did feel like part of a family there for those years. That's what separates this franchise from all the rest. The history, the pursuit of greatness—but most of all—the feeling of family.

ACKNOWLEDGMENTS

A special thanks to Fred Gaudelli, who at different times taught both authors the ins and outs of sports television. And a nod to Chris Pfeiffer, who worked with both of us separately and thought to put us together on this endeavor. And we can't forget our editor, Jeff Fedotin, who made the whole process a pleasure.

Jim Kaat

Thank you to Bob Zellner, station owner of KSMM in Shakopee, Minnesota, who hired me on his 500-watt daytime station to experience everything from livestock reports, spinning records, and doing high school sports and to legendary sportscasters Ray Scott, Merle Harmon, and Herb Carneal for listening to and critiquing those early attempts at sports broadcasting.

Thanks to ESPN for hiring me to do college baseball in their early years and Bill White, who was my mentor and helped me so much when I announced Yankees games on WPIX in 1986. Thank you to Michael Weisman at NBC and Glenn Diamond at TBS for opportunities to do games. Ted Shaker was the executive producer who told me to be patient when I read some of the big names considered for an analyst position at CBS. He was true to his word, and I got the assignment. Thank you Bob McCann at WCCO in Minneapolis for hiring me to do Twins games, Tony Kubek for recommending me to MSG Network, and then to Mike McCarthy, the best boss an announcer could have, for hiring me. If not for Howard Katz, vice president at ESPN, who allowed me to leave in the middle of my contract to get back to the ballpark and leave the studio, I wouldn't have been able to go to MSG.

Thank you Dick Enberg and Dick Stockton for helping me learn the art and Harry Coyle, the legendary director, for giving me the formula for announcing a game. Thank you to Fred Gaudelli when he was at ESPN for urging me to sit in the production truck and learn what goes into a telecast and how to use the talk back key and the timing of announcing a game properly.

Thank you to Leo Hindery at YES when they started the network and Russell Gabay of MLB International, who convinced me I needed to get back in the booth after MaryAnn passed away in 2008 and hired me to do the WBC, and that led to Tony Pettiti giving me a chance to work with Bob Costas and Matt Vasgersian and Chris Pfeiffer and his production crew at the MLB Network.

Greg Jennings

A s for all those who have helped hone my craft to the point where I had enough confidence to take on this task, I should single out Brian Brown and Aaron Cohen. You guys set such a high bar that just thinking about trying to reach it improves my game. To Bruce Jaffe and the late Lou Saracco: the two guys who really taught me how to write, one history paper at a time. And special thanks to Esther Blum for taking me through the process of writing a book and giving me the courage to take that leap.

I also need to tip my hat to my parents, Russ and Carole, for taking me to Yankees and Mets games growing up, not to mention all those little league games. My love of baseball comes from their dedication. And to my kids, Madison, Kortney, and Gavin, for both letting Daddy work and for making him play.

And finally, to my wife, Kelly, for taking on all the extra responsibilities to give me the time to write this book. These pages are as much yours as they are mine.

SOURCES

Books

Araton, Harvey, *Driving Mr. Yogi,* First Mariner Books, 2013

Green, Ron Jr., *101 Reasons to Love the Yankees.* A Tiegreen Book, 2008, revised edition

Kaat, Jim, with Pepe, Phil, *Still Pitching: Musings from the Mound and the Microphone.* Triumph Books, 2003

Lyle, Sparky and Golenbock, Peter, *The Bronx Zoo: The Astonishing Inside Story of the 1978 World Champion New York Yankees.* Triumph Books, 2005

O'Connor, Ian, *The Captain: The Journey of Derek Jeter.* First Mariner Books, 2012

Rivera, Mariano, with Coffey, Wayne, *The Closer.* Little Brown and Co., 2014

Shannon, Mike, *Tales from the Dugout: The Greatest True Baseball Stories Ever Told.* McGraw-Hill, 1997

Videos

Baseball: A Film by Ken Burns, 2010

The House of Steinbrenner ESPN Films, 30 for 30, 2010

Nine Innings from Ground Zero HBO, 2004

Websites

1995Mariners.com

Baseball-Almanac.com

BaseballLibrary.com

Baseball-Reference.com

BleacherReport.com

Bleedingyankeeblue.blogspot.com

Bloomberg.com

BostonGlobe.com

LATimes.com

LouGehrig.com

NewYork.Yankeesmlb.com

Forums.nyyfans.com

NYDailyNews.com

NYPost.com

NYTimes.com

Retrosheet.org

Sabr.org

SI.com

Stltoday.com

USATODAY.com